LIGHTNESS

ILKKA SUPPANEN

DESIGN

Lars Müller Publishers

I wanted to make a book that delves into the essence of lightness—
a phenomenon that has consistently shaped my work as a designer.
To for the first time talk about this through my work, and simultaneously
include different perspectives to gain better knowledge about it.

LIGHTNESS
ILKKA SUPPANEN

Introduction

Light——Transformation of Elements

Sara Heinämaa

Ancient Greek philosophers explained the world and the cosmos in terms of basic elements. Usually, they distinguished between four such principles: earth, water, fire and air. However, some bold thinkers argued that it is enough to postulate just one or two fundamental elements and explain all experienceable phenomena as combinations of their properties and powers. The boldest of all, Aristotle, thought that a fifth element—sensing flesh—is needed to account for the perceptual activities of living beings and, among them, for the power of the human eye.

Light was also considered in terms of the basic elements, not as an element itself but as a modification or transformation that the radiant element of fire was able to bring about in the other elements. The Ancients thought that the transparent elements of water and air filled the space between the seeing eye and the visible thing. Fire, emanating from various light sources—the sun, the moon, burning torches and the intelligent eye—entered the transparent elements and illuminated everything that found its place within them.

So, space was never empty for the Ancients but was always occupied by some element or other. The transparent and potentially radiant element of air filled all intervals between solid grounds and distant skies, extending over the valleys, canyons and caverns that formed ever deeper places on the Earth. The heavier element of water meanwhile occupied the spaces that lay lower and closer to the Earth's core. It spread from oceans and lakes to streams, rivers and brooks, and formed living environments for the many creatures who depended on and enjoyed the watery element.

The fiery element was able to illuminate all such spaces and places and all beings in them. It operated by mixing with the transparent elements of air and water, and thereby activating the potential visibility that lay in their essence and in the essences of the visible things and creatures that were bound together by the elements. So, each dawn the fire of the morning sun threw its light on the waters and the atmospheres that filled all places under the skies, and by illuminating these elements, it also illuminated the things and creatures who lived in them.

Fire operated by actualizing the visibility of these beings and thus allowed the seeing eye to catch sight of them. Alone it was relatively powerless, but with the intermediate elements and the sensing moving eyes of living animals, it was able to activate seeing and disclose the visible.

We late moderns have lost sight of illumination and enlightenment. We are trained to imagine phenomena as mere impacts in endless chains of causes and effects and are accustomed to conceiving the universe as a closed network of such chains. Our space is forever empty, and all the elementary particles that we are interested in and capable of knowing—atoms, electrons and quarks—are utterly inert and hopelessly colorless.

This physicalist and positivist framework is supposed to also govern our own visions and all the visible things, events and processes that we and others are able to capture. To our detriment, the universal network of inert causes and effects should even explain the work of visionaries, the people who are able look forward in time and notice signs of coming things.

However, according to the late modern account, vision and insight are merely effects of electromagnetic waves on the neural networks of some organisms. There are properly speaking no seers and no visionaries.

For a philosophical visionary, it seems that this modern account of vision has reached its limits and that the time has come to revive the latter understanding, the ancient one.

A backward glance at ancient discussions on the phenomena of light will help us to renew our notions of enlightenment. Rather than being modelled on the computational techniques of information-processes, fact-gathering and data mining, human insight can, once again, be cultivated as a dynamic power of experiencing, exploring and examining. As such it refers us to what happens outside the mind-brain in the world.

The operations of minds thus enlightened will be light in two related senses of the word. On the one hand lucid and perspicuous, and thereby capable of illuminating whatever remains vague, gloomy and dark. But also, weightless and nimble, even light-hearted, since they will be free from the weight of escalating facts and dissimilating causes and therefore capable of observing vast landscapes and transcending their horizons.

Gestures

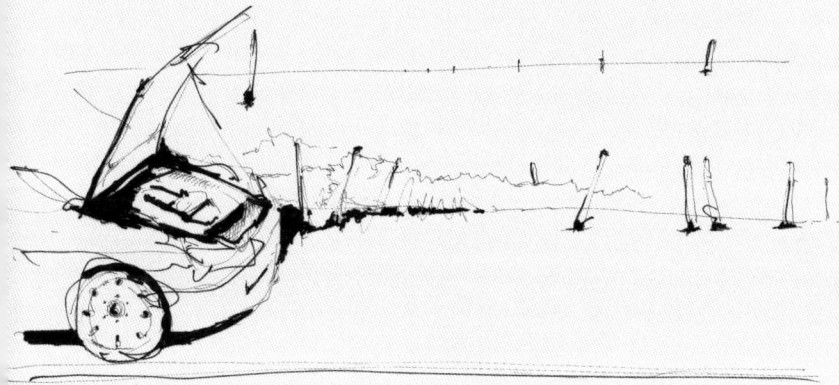

There exists an elegant subtlety in everyday experiences, where lightness materializes before us in the form of nuanced gestures. These gestures often go unnoticed, a feature which paradoxically forms their core intention. Their beauty lies in their inconspicuousness, their ability to operate "under the radar" while still influencing a situation. These minimal gestures, despite their apparent invisibility, contribute in a meaningful way to our daily interactions. Without overwhelming the existing scenario, they offer gentle guidance, subtle warnings, or convey crucial messages. Like simple manners or an open hood on a car by the side of the road.

The technical brief stated that this product should be easily mailed, and so we departed from the largest European standard mailbox size and quite pragmatically worked our way backward. I landed on the decision to design a vase. This idea was influenced by a memory of my mother. She came from a very simple background and always told me that it is not the quantity that counts, it is the quality. We often used to walk together in the woods where we lived in Finland, and she would talk about and show me all the different plants. She would always pick one piece to bring home where she arranged it in a nice way on the table, immediately making the room feel richer. It did not necessarily have to be a flower, it could be a single straw or some kind of reed, something which when you see in abundance you do not really register, but when seen on its own is beautiful. So this product is a combination of my mother's poetic way of looking at and appreciating the environment, and an extreme consideration for the size of an object. The glass is actually a test tube, commonly found in laboratories. Meanwhile the structure, which can be dismantled relatively easily, is made alternatively from steel, copper or gold. The outline creates a volume that is reminiscent of a larger vase and the material and composition combined makes it a beautiful object in its own right.

One
vase, be & liv
2015

When I was first asked to design for Muuto, this company really only existed on a piece of paper. The persons behind it had a vision to create a new contemporary brand that was not just about celebrating the heritage of Scandinavian design, but also its present. And even though they had no track record in the industry, I felt that this was intriguing and wanted to help and be a part of it. Luckily, they became very successful. So, in one way—with hard work obviously—what you hope for sometimes happens. What they specifically wanted me to design was a coffee mug, which resulted in this glazed ceramic piece. If you consider coffee culture in the past, especially in the Nordics and Northern America, the coffee mug is the result of a perhaps less advanced coffee culture based on consuming large amounts. This stands in contrast to the let us say more sophisticated coffee culture found in the south. But then there was a revolution within the world of coffee and eventually you could get even an espresso at a gas station far up in the north. To me at least, the generic coffee mug still represents this old northern way of having your coffee. I decided to merge the two coffee cultures into one object and designed a mug that appears to have a smaller cup joined together with a larger cup. You can fill up the bottom with a small amount of coffee, or if you prefer, fill it up generously. Its shape makes an ear or handle obsolete. The name of this mug might feel like a contradiction, given its intended use, but another way to look at it is that the coffee break is actually a holy moment for some. In Scandinavia we even have a law that permits us to a fifteen-minute coffee break, which is a wonderful thing because everyday things like this really can make a difference in your life.

Everyday Holy Mug
Muuto
2004

Wristwatch
Mazoni & Fils
2010

To read a watch from a cultural point of view is interesting. A watch is a small signal to any person in your vicinity that you can get the time from that person if you ask them for it. The watch on your wrist is also a status symbol, because we do not need it to tell the time anymore since there are many devices around us which already serve as timepieces. A watch tells you something about a person, or we believe that it does. It becomes like an extension of a need, a need to buy into a preferred character that shows what you would like others to think about you. At the same time, I believe it works the other way around. Our identity is not always so clear. I know my name is Ilkka, but who am I? Sometimes I want to have a confirmation that I am a serious designer, so I put on a certain watch and a white shirt to confirm it to myself. I only do it for me—if it is correct or not, I do not know. This is a mechanical watch made in Switzerland and, in that world, there is not much room to innovate as the design is the result of a long tradition where all the aspects have already been carefully figured out. What you can do as a designer is to change parameters such as graphics, shape, color or finish. It was an amazing experience to see how these watches are made. Despite the help of a lot of machinery it is nevertheless in the end very much a product of manual labor. A millimeter is a huge distance in this small universe and becomes so important that you must recalibrate your brain and eyes to understand what to pay attention to. This watch tells you the time and date. It also shows the circulation of the Moon around the Earth which makes you realize that our calendar is kind of fucked. We have 28, 30 and 31 days in a month, yet the Moon does not follow this. It is quite fascinating that within this object you are measuring the movement of our solar system. This makes you think about the different scales of time which are related to the circulation of the Earth around the Sun, and around itself. The one dominating idea of the design was to make the case and dial in such a shape that it would be clearly readable from a distance. The case is shaped like a pebble found on a beach, which I know is a worn-out reference but nonetheless true. I in fact always find myself collecting rocks or stones that have been given beautiful shapes by the forces of nature over time.

Everyday Wedding Ring
personal project
2003

This story originates from meeting the American fiber artist Sheila Hicks. I was visiting her studio in Paris, France, and she gave me a piece of gold-plated thread. This thread was extremely fragile, and one could easily snap it in two with one's fingers. For a while it lay on my desk, where it became like a stress toy that I picked up whenever I was on the phone. One day I subconsciously spun it around my finger and thought that it actually looked like a nice ring. I wanted to show this to my girlfriend, but before I made it home it had broken. My girlfriend at the time had been married once before and her standpoint on the issue was that it was a bad idea because you truly cannot commit to somebody for the rest of your life since tomorrow is unknown. It was a discussion we had, and my standpoint was the opposite. I argued that there is a beauty in a commitment, there is beauty in committing to anything even if you do not know what will happen tomorrow. We had different ideas about it, but it was not a problem in our relationship, it was more an interesting way to talk about relationships in general, and one that I guess many couples have. So, when I got home and had lost the ring it struck me that it would be the perfect wedding ring for our relationship. We could commit to each other with this ring because it would be gone by the end of the day. We then got the choice to recommit again in the morning—a constant marriage that allows you to skip a day or two. Sometime later this ring was actually used in a real wedding.

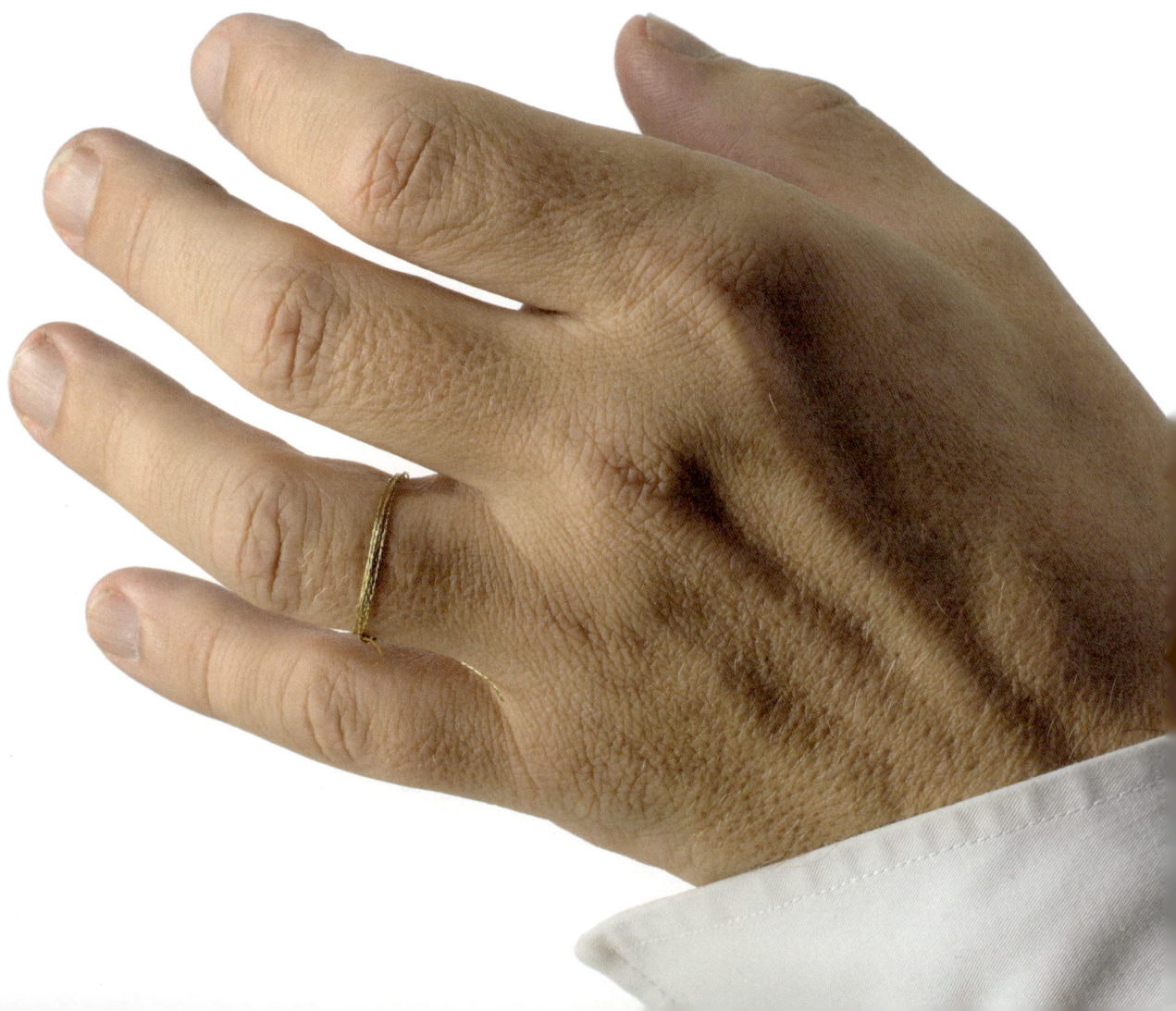

The Lightness of Gestures

———

Stefana Broadbent

When we dwell on the lightness of gestures, the word "graceful" immediately springs to mind. The movements of dancers or artists are of course graceful, but we also recognize grace in gestures such as shaping an object or using a tool. We see the beauty of the hands molding clay or slicing a fish, when the movements are artful and minimal. We are irked by the heaviness and excess of the unskilled hand, the imprecision of an act, the unneeded effort or the waste of material. As observers we recognize the seamless and frictionless nature of gestures that have been acquired by long practice and learning, which become at once essential and seemingly effortless. We instinctively realize that the gesture no longer needs conscious control and that the action flows naturally, with the focus of attention on the changing environment rather than on the internal mechanisms that control the execution of the movement. When a gesture has been mastered, the focus can move onto the object and onto the variations that can be introduced when one interacts with it. Trained musicians can introduce a very slight contrast in the pressure of a key to produce a faintly different sound or rhythm, because the sequence of their movements has been so fully mastered that it no longer fully requires their attention. The same happens to craftspeople such as glass-blowers, who no longer need to focus on their breathing or the rotation of their hand but can slightly modify the tilt of their rolling of the glass on a surface to obtain a different shape or color. What makes watching skillful people so mesmerizing is the fact that their gestures become nearly invisible, and our attention is drawn to how the material interacts with them.

The anthropologist Tim Ingold talks of "enskillment" and the relation between knowledge, gestures and the environment.[1] Acquired gestures are not a set of prescriptive routines which have been memorized, but are rather part of a growing attunement to the environment, which itself is acquired by learning the most important and relevant elements of information to which one should become attuned. In other words, the skillful potter is capable of feeling and seeing movements and textures in the clay that produce minute variations of the gestures of the hand. When we observe skillful craftspeople or artists, we are in awe of their coupling with their materials.

1=Tim Ingold, "The Perception of the User–Producer," in *Design and Anthropology*, Abingdon, 2016, pp. 19–34.

Anthropology teaches us that gestures and behaviors are rarely the product of an individual's invention, but are rather social and cultural in origin. The crafts that involve the mastery of gestures are most often acquired by apprenticeship and practice, where a skilled teacher demonstrates how to hold, cut, rotate and shape, stimulating imitation and demanding practice and repetition. The gestures taught have emerged from a long process of making them more essential, effective and efficient: the best way of bending an arm or of holding a tool, of tying a knot. This cultural transmission also focuses on imparting the relevant elements of the materials to observe, such as the changing color, texture, smell, vibration or temperature. These crafts are patiently taught so that new apprentices do not need to themselves reinvent the craft and repeat the mistakes of the past: all the movements that went wrong, that broke the glass and the clay, that split the wood or sounded off-tune. In other words, transmitting cultural gestures involves transmitting the long quest for lightness of the many people in the past who have engaged in a craft.

But we should not forget that skills and crafts are nearly always also mediated by tools and artefacts which themselves have long histories and multiple variations, each embedding the knowledge and skill of people who came before us. Edwin Hutchins, who studied the navigation of the Micronesian people, the navigation instruments of the US Navy, and the cockpits of commercial airlines,[2] shows how maps, electronic compasses or digital bearings embed complex measurements and computations that allow the sailors and captains to quickly identify their position without reinventing a system of coordinates or of speed. In the same way, the shape of a knife or a rake have been honed over centuries to offer the best angle to cut into the scales of a tuna fish or into the sand of a garden. The clasp to hold the clay lightly, the string to tie, the bow, the sail, the rake or the brush are all tools that have been tried, modified, redesigned and tried again in order to best support the way a gesture performs on a material or an environment. Skilled craftspeople, artists or sportspeople always bring their finely-tuned instruments, because the tools are integral part of their movements; and as anthropologists would say, they are aware that their actions are situated rather than confined within their individual brains and bodies; that their skills

2=Edwin Hutchins, *Cognition in the Wild*, Cambridge, MA, 1995.

are immanent to the relations and transformations supported by their tools, their materials and the environments with which they engage.

Just as we appreciate graceful gestures, we also recognize graceful artefacts. As with movements, the grace here comes from the essentiality of an artefact. This is the feeling it conveys that it is the product of many, many cycles of experimentation to dispel the useless and retain the effective. This process of dispelling ensures the lightness of essentiality, which does not necessarily entail functionalism, but simply the progressive identification of what is important. A machine with thousands of pieces can be as light and graceful as a brush. What makes it light is not its simplicity, but the capacity to enable a successful coupling between people and their environment. The cognitive archeologist Lambros Malafouris, talking of the use of flints by early hominids, writes that:

> All thinking happens where the hand meets the stone. Perception, memory, attention, intention, estimation, expectation, prediction and anticipation take the form of a dialogue between the maker and the material that sometimes agrees and sometime resists. Every act of making (not just the making of a stone tool) is an act of collaboration between the agency of human bodies and the agency of materials, reflecting a world where the neural side of the mental domain is constantly shaped and negotiated by the force of the hand and the affordances of the stone.[3]

In other words, light tools and artefacts not only support skilled gestures but also skilled thoughts, ways of thinking that bring the interaction between humans and their environments into balance.

3=Lambros Malafouris, "How Does Thinking Relate to Tool Making?," *Adaptive Behavior* 29, no. 2 (2021): 1–15, here p. 11.

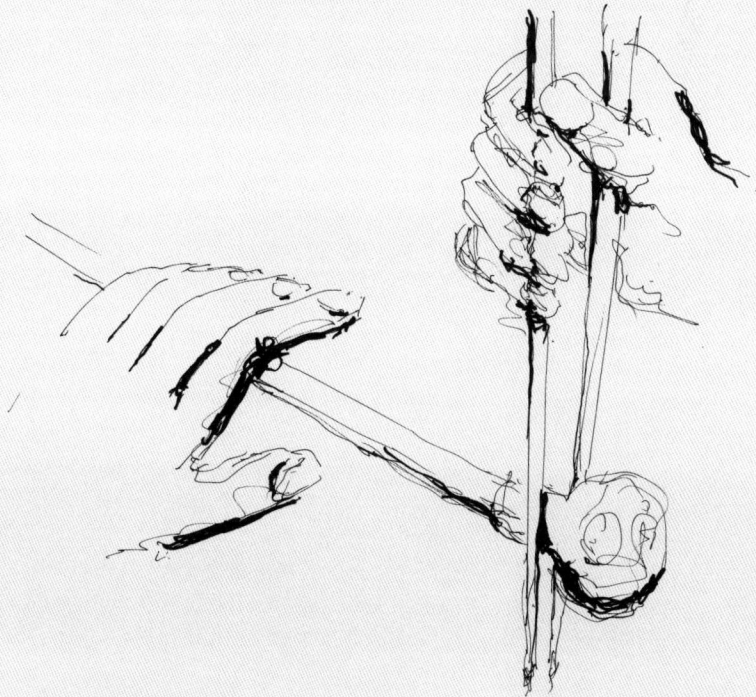

Materials

Material innovations within the arts and industry transform the landscape of design and affect the way we experience and interact with the world around us. It is not just the development of novel materials that have catalyzed these changes, but also new applications of old and existing materials: Reinforced concrete—originally patented to make flowerpots—several decades later enabled architects to make pillar and beam structures to liberate walls and façades from load-bearing constraints, effectively rendering the façade as merely a curtain; carbon fiber and even wood compounds can facilitate the construction of larger and more efficient blades on windmills; meanwhile technological textiles makes moon walks in space possible.

Loco

prototype for bag, Snowcrash
2001

Maybe it all began with the prehistoric hunter-gatherer, but throughout the ages different kinds of bags have been essential to our survival and prosperity. At the last millennium shift, when the Internet, mobile phones and laptops started to become widely available, there was a moment where we adapted to a new nomadic lifestyle that felt rather immediate. For a while people did not know where to put this new digital gear, and that kind of situation was exactly what occupied the minds of the Finnish design collective Snowcrash (1997–2003) of whom I was a part. I imagined a bag that was not just a simple container, but more like a toolbox, an idea not that distant from the rolled-up piece of cloth with wrenches that people used to keep in the trunk of their car. Loco would hold everything in place, and when opened, you could work directly out of it like a portable miniature office—a typology of bags that became relevant in almost everybody's daily life, and still is.

Porcupine
lamps,
Galerie Maria Wettergren
2007

As part of a group of Finnish designers I was asked by the Japanese company Lisn to think of new concepts for incense holders. A small product with a long history, commonly used in the temple and the home, it holds a stick that gives off a cleansing pillar of sweet smoke while it slowly burns. Sometimes it is the production technique that becomes the vehicle that leads to innovation rather than the actual material. Accordingly, I used this occasion to experiment and try to understand the logic behind a new technology that was emerging at the time: 3D printing. It promised a revolution in manufacturing because it allows you to create shapes that would be almost impossible to make in any other way. It is controlled by a computer and so it does not matter if a line is straight or curved, it is all the same cost, time and calculation. This allows you to think in new ways about the object you design. A plastic powder is hardened with a laser, and this means that you calculate the material differently. Instead of a reductive process wherein you take away mass to give an object its shape, you use an additive process which leaves no waste. So being rational about this you try and have as little volume as possible to create maximum effect. I eventually made two holders for an exhibition with the company, but afterwards felt that I had to continue my experiment. I kept the shape I had designed but pushed the limits of the size since the size of the printing machine really is the only parameter that puts any restrain to your creation. My further work resulted in Porcupine, a floor and pendant lamp in copper and plastics for Maria Wettergren Gallery in Paris, France. 3D printing is a fascinating technology that keeps on evolving and that changes the way we talk about labor and the role of the craftsperson. But really the craftsperson remains the same, only the environment has changed. The hands that would formerly be dirtied from handling a material now get dirty from working the keyboard, and both ways demands expertise and knowledge, which is the result of the experience of trying and failing.

To be able to sail is one of humankind's most remarkable innovations, so much in our history is a result of it, travelling to new continents—you can even argue that capitalism was developed through the fact that somebody was able to bring something from a far-off place on a ship and sell it for profit. I have sailed most of my life and I am still amazed that with skill and technology you can make such a huge amount of mass float and move in a desired direction, without consuming any energy besides wind and water. Sails gradually became made of a synthetic textile, different kinds of composites, and the ratio they follow is that it should be as strong as possible with as little weight as possible. These technological textiles are appreciated for their performance rather than aesthetic. But you look at a material differently when you use it in another way than it had originally been for, and this often leads to opportunities in other contexts. In architecture, ceilings in public spaces are quite demanding because they hold several complex parts such as ventilation tubes, electrical cables and sprinkler systems. In many cases these parts are left more or less visible for economic reasons even though it is not necessarily pleasing to look at. The idea for Hi Wave was therefore to offer two solutions in one—act like a suspended ceiling and a light. Large sheets of synthetic sail cloth are upheld with thin metal rods which diffuses the light source in an unexpected way while it offers an unusual spatial experience.

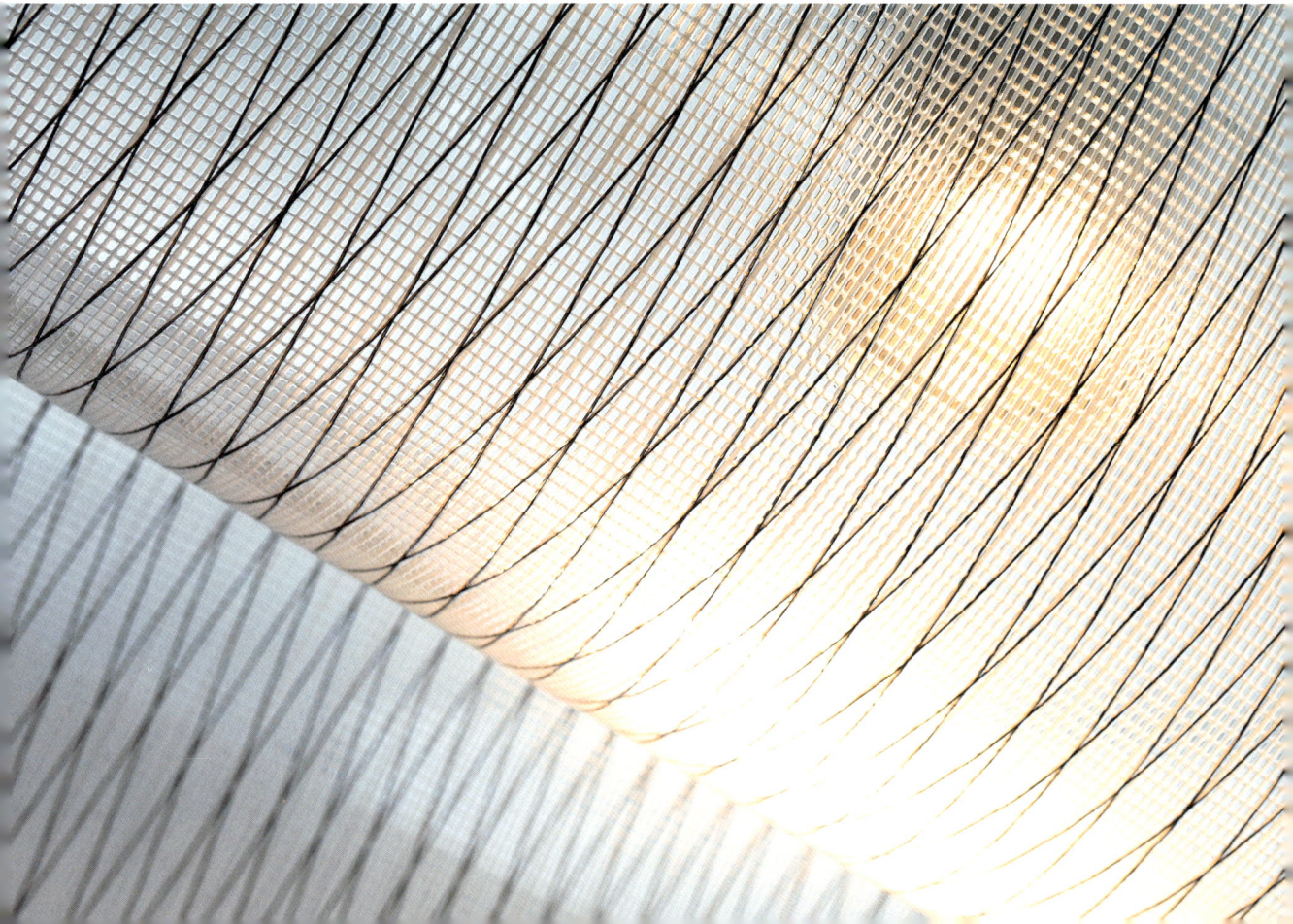

Hi Wave
lamps, Snowcrash
1998

The furniture industry, of which I am a part, is quite conservative when it comes to using materials that are developed in other industries and for other purposes. We normally use the conventional variety of wood, plastics, metal and textiles even though other variations clearly can offer new possibilities. The material is everything for some furniture—as with Airbag. It is made out of materials developed for camping and sports gear, the fabric used for the floor in tents, and the belts used for bags containing equipment. Their mechanical and technical durability are critical so they can resist the stress they will be submitted to by different weather conditions and bodies. In one way Airbag is a direct development of the original Sacco chair, which I have always admired. It is difficult to think of a more comfortable chair, as it uses minimal material and still gives you so much comfort. Plastic balls together with trapped air create a softness that you shape with your body. And we merely sought to evolve this so that the shape could be controlled in a sitting position. But if we would not have gotten our hands on the unconventional material to begin with, we probably never would have designed this furniture at all; it would not be what it is, it would feel and function differently.

Airbag
seating furniture,
with Pasi Kolhonen,
Snowcrash
1997

Saab
concept car
1997

Since the 1950s there has been a tradition of car fairs where manufacturers test the market's reaction to their new designs. Here they present what is called "concept cars"— a vision of the car of the future. Oftentimes, this is not even a car that works, but it looks like it does, so people can understand it better. In the 1990s, when the Swedish company Saab was still making cars, I was hired to develop an interior concept for an existing model called the Saab 9-3 cabriolet. At this moment I had recently learned about a temporary cast technique used for emergencies. When a skier falls on a slope and breaks something, that person needs to get down the hill safely. So, when the sledge or helicopter arrives, the broken limb is placed on a bag filled with small soft balls. The air is then sucked out of the bag which hardens and forms a perfect shape around the leg or arm, so it can rest in a secured position. My idea was to use this technology in the seats of the car where it could be activated simply by pressing a button. A person resting in a moving vehicle is a dynamic situation and therefore the prospect of applying this technique was a valid and thrilling idea. However, it never made it to the car fair.

Material and Lightness

―――――

Dai Fujiwara

"Material" equals thought, "lightness" equals measurement
When I think of "material," I tend to visualize a final product. When I see it, I want to touch it and know its origins. I try to visualize the final product to see what can be done with the material. Then, I think about the actions required, and finally, I think about the meaning of the whole thing. I believe that whether something is considered a "material" is related to human desire or ego. For example, let's say you're walking in a forest with a friend. Straight twigs on the ground might just be sticks to one person, and material for chopsticks to the other.

"Material" consists of three interconnected circles:
> 1. "Things" (物) that supports daily life
> 2. "Events" (事) that influence human behavior
> 3. "Meanings" (意味) that affect human psychology

What about "lightness"? A unit for measuring weight first comes to mind. But besides physical objects, lightness can also measure events and meanings. People gauge the "lightness" of the things, events and meanings derived from "materials" as mentioned above as a measure of intelligence. Thus, words have multiple meanings. Time also seems to play a role. Let's explore this further.

Dissecting material and lightness
"Material" (from the Latin *mater*, meaning "mother") likens nature, where materials originate, to a mother. In Japanese "material" is called *sozai*, while in Chinese, it's *sùcái*. Given China's historical influence on Japan, the two countries share many common etymologies. *Sozai* breaks into two parts: *so* and *zai*. *So* originated in ancient China and was derived from a pictograph meaning "sheep's wool." It refers to the cloth made by weaving sheep's wool. Then, clothes were made and worn for various purposes. By extension, it also means "white," which symbolizes cleanliness and purity. Thus, *so* became widely used in Japan to convey human emotions. Over time, its meanings multiplied, and the word became multi-dimensional. *Zai* means lumber or raw material, and it also carries the meanings of talent and ability. It is the material used for making things after the tree has been cut down. It has also come to mean the ability and talent of the person who uses the lumber. Thus, *zai* spans both physical and

abstract meanings. *Kei* means "lightness" in Japanese, and is a familiar term for the Japanese. For instance, it refers to the smallest type of car most Japanese mother's drive. This notion also ties into the etymology of the word in Chinese, originating from the lightweight yet swift movement of ancient war chariots.

Over time, the scale of "lightness" became finer and more precise, and the concept of "lightness" expanded to measure not just physical weight but also the relative importance of situations and intangible, psychological aspects. The reason that "lightness" has come to include such a variety of meanings is that society's intelligence is growing increasingly sophisticated.

The equivalence of mass and energy

Einstein's principle of mass—energy equivalence has greatly influenced our understanding of lightness and materials. For example, helium, the second lightest element in the universe, offers excellent insulation if used to wrap a house. Helium is made up of two protons and two neutrons, thus four subatomic particles in total. The weight of the four subatomic particles and their combined weight as one atom of helium ought to be the same, but helium is lighter. Einstein's surprising conclusion was that "mass is a form of energy." Let's apply this law to human activity. Who uses more energy: a person who belongs to a group such as a company, cooperative or state that gathers intelligence or an individual who does not belong to any group (there are very few of these in the world)? The energy consumed by groups to bring people together must be greater than that used by individuals working on their own. For example, groups build offices and cities. Does this mean that people who belong to groups are heavier than individuals who do not belong to a group? If so, is the invisible energy of groups exacting a price from nature? And what about the lightness?

Waterfalls

Let me end by comparing my life to a waterfall. My house sits on a mountain with many stairs. If you come over in high heels, your feet will be cramped. There is no road for cars or motorbikes. So, when we go shopping, we look for the lightest materials. I walk every day to carry the food and household goods I need for my life. My wife and children do the same. My problem? Potatoes, onions, cabbages and carrots—heavy materials that I'm in charge of. The materials I bring disappear from our kitchen like a waterfall, flowing through our bodies and down the mountain via the sewer. One day, I secretly had these items delivered via Amazon. It lightened both my work and my mind—and my wallet too. This is the law of equivalence of mass and energy at work. However, using delivery services gives me pause. I suspect this dilemma exists worldwide. As we seek "lightness," we require ideas, technology, people, energy and funds, and these things and events, intertwined with meaning, circulate through our lives.

The Dutch artist Maurits Cornelis Escher magnificently depicted the concept of a perpetual cycle in his lithographs. The trompe-l'œil image of water falling from a waterfall and reversing to the top again symbolizes a perpetual motion machine. The water is clear, light and pure, much like the essence of "so." If you flip the "m" in "mater" to a "w," it becomes "water." Yet I believe that natural water, the epitome of purity, has long evaporated from the world. What circulates now is the pure desire of humans. In this way, "material" expands the space of human intelligence, while "lightness" measures it. The relationship between material and lightness accentuates and unifies the properties of both things and events. Together they provide meaning to our society and our Earth.

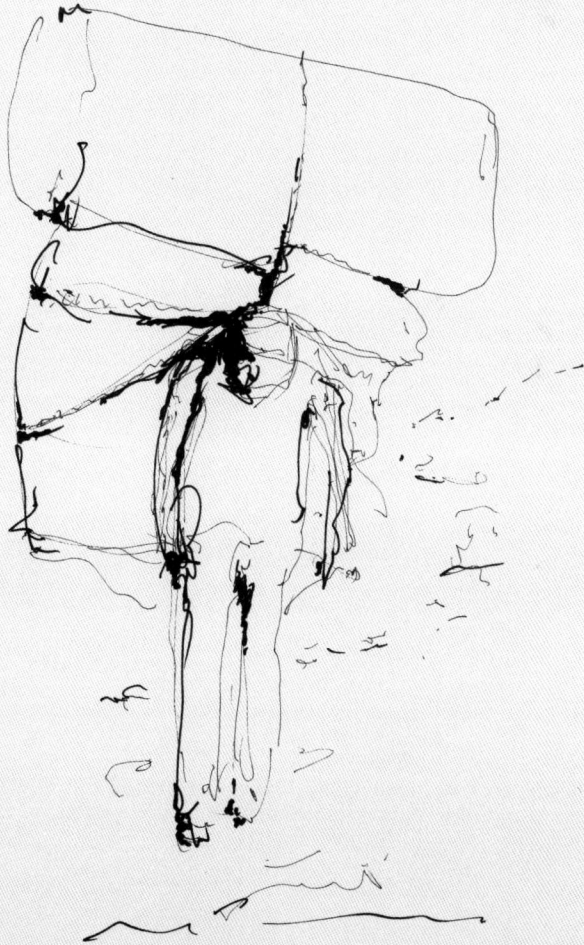

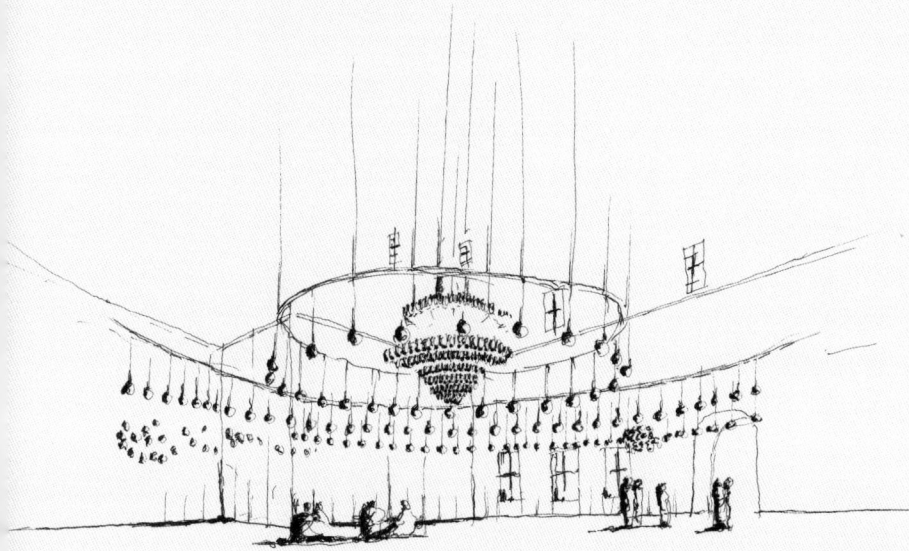

The German philosopher Immanuel Kant (1724–1804) proposed that our experience of lightness is inherently subjective, shaped and defined by our individual perceptions of light. It is through light that most of us perceive and understand our reality. Light offers a unique medium for creative exploration, we can control its intensity, direction and color, which grants us the power to manipulate and design our surroundings. In essence, light defines our aesthetic experiences. As in Baroque church architecture, or the design of a mosque, wherein space is defined by light and shadow instead of color or texture. We can also think of how the effects of light were created on canvases by the Impressionist painters.

Someone next to me can say that a glass piece looks dull, and I can understand why it does for several reasons. When it comes to glass—and this is something I have come to realize over the years—there are two dominant phenomena that define what we see in the surface of the glass and that affect its aesthetic qualities. One is the reflection; glass partly reflects the surroundings you are in. The other is the refraction; glass changes the direction of light when it travels through its mass. If you look at Darya you see different shapes, but the colors and shadows you see are what surround this object, which in the case of this photo is the space behind the photographer. When you work with a piece like this, with all its different parts, you have to bear in mind that you are not only working with glass but also with light—how it affects the expression beyond the color and texture of the physical object. It is not fully possible to calculate how this plays out, but you can learn that aspects such as shapes, colors, thickness and mirroring all give different desired effects.

Darya
unique glass piece,
Galerie Forsblom
2019

Kaasa
tealight candleholder,
Iittala
2015

Kaasa is an old Finnish word for the fires that were set up along the shoreline to help sailors at sea navigate safely. Basically, an early version of a lighthouse. Colored light became used throughout the global marine world to recognize where something is. A ship has a green light on its right side and a red on its left, and that way someone watching it from afar can instantly understand in which direction it is heading. Colored light gives a strong association to safety in general, from exit lights to blenders on the top of firetrucks, ambulances and police cars. The safety regulations for candle products are very strict and they change almost annually between markets. So, by designing a metal base that does not transfer heat from the candle to the colored glass dome that protects the light from the wind, this tealight holder is an extremely safe addition to this vast product segment. And that is why Kaasa felt like the best name for it.

This pendant lamp is composed of one plastic part that is repeated to create a shade around its light source. Using only one part has kept the mold cost down, and the plastic can be either clear or colored. In this product the way the light behaves is fairly predictable and it is easy for the viewer to understand how the light works with the material. Differing thickness and the direction of the material make the light sometimes reflect back to the viewer and sometimes go through the material, and this creates a variation in glance with darkness and highlights on the surface.

Canary
lamps, Koizumi
2009

Kai
unique glass piece
2019

Kai consists of a glass shade with a blue gradient, that holds a small mirror glass ball on the inside. These surfaces play together in the light, a technique called "mirroring," and one which I use in many of my glass pieces. We all see mirrors daily and these are most likely made of an aluminum or steel sheet that has been industrially polished and then covered with a clear piece of glass to protect the surface. Early versions of mirrors were made on the island of Murano in Venice, and the way they did it was to treat a surface with silver nitrate. This was expensive and so these mirrors were more likely to end up in the Palace of Versailles than in a countryside farmhouse. Mirrors like these are still handmade in Murano, and that is also how the ball for Kai was made. If you ever get the chance to compare you will be amazed—the mirror in silver and the mirror in aluminum give two surprisingly different reflections of reality.

This lampshade, which is made in versions for table, floor and pendant lamps, consists of two glass parts. The top part is in white. It is the kind of milky white shade that you are likely to find somewhere in any room you enter. Looking straight at a lightbulb is blinding, it is a lot of light coming from one small point. One way to deal with this is to dim the light source, but that will mean less light to illuminate your space which might not have been the intention. So, the basic idea of a shade like this, beyond the aesthetics, is to have the same amount of light coming from a larger surface so it will not blind you. The lower part of Bisquit is a clear glass piece. Since it is attached to the top piece, which holds the light source, light moves through it and out at the bottom, creating a thin circle of light. And since you do not see the light source, this effect appears almost like magic.

Bisquit
lamp collection, Leucos
2006

Sea, Suppanen, and Sun

———

Max Borka

Ilkka Suppanen and Albert Einstein have more in common than their flowing manes. Key to both of their work is above all a preoccupation with light. Einstein, son of a pioneering but failed electric light dealer, elevated light to the only constant in the universe, relegating time and space to the status of variables. Suppanen's passion for light in all the meanings of the word, is meanwhile closely linked to his being a keen sailor—an enthusiasm which he also shares with Einstein. No coincidence. A compact boat forces one to travel light. And light itself is used as a navigation tool, from the starry sky, the beacons and lighthouses, to electric green and red bulbs—all essential to survival. These have all served him as examples when designing.

To survive and defuse the growth of Protestantism and the Reformation, from the sixteenth century onwards the Catholic Church built churches that heightened the mesmerizing effect of the starry sky. Baroque architects used elements from the Renaissance, such as domes and colonnades, but made them bigger and higher, and more dramatically decorated with trompe l'oeils and *quadratura*, ceiling paintings which depicted the firmament. Twisted columns and large "stairways to heaven" enhanced upwards motion. Light streamed down from cupolas, reflecting in an abundance of gilding. From Italy the Baroque style then spread lightning fast, and even generated a palace such as Versailles. It became a turning point in history. Light was no longer just a means to observe and understand reality, but—through its intensity, color and direction—became pivotal in changing it. Light became a design tool.

Baroque exuberance is generally not for Finns. But Ilkka Suppanen lives in Finland and Italy, and he loves both. His parents even lived in Jordan for a while, making him a man shaped by both Scandinavian and Arab influences. They are kinda samesame. For what is a desert but a sea without water? At night, both act as a vast pedestal for that overwhelming starry sky. But they are also opposites. While in the north people forage most of the year to bring in the scarce light, in the Arab world it is mainly a matter of keeping abundant sunlight out of interior spaces. To accomplish this, Arab architects can fall back on a rich architectural tradition, based on ancient, low-tech typologies that are still novel in the rest of the world. For example, in ancient Yemeni architecture light was cleverly interwoven with ventilation and heat control, in techniques that are still examples of best practices in sustainability and energy-efficiency. Such techniques also varied the height and width differences between buildings and streets in cities to create shade, and determined the design of the famous windows allowing light to be brought in decoratively through *Qamariyah* fanlights and *Mashrabiya*. Through these structures, light became aesthetics. Above all: it became lightness, minimal.

The ways in which light's poetry can transcend gravity are even demonstrated in as unlikely a place as the Alabaster Mosque, built in Cairo in the first half of the nineteenth century, and another inspiration for Ilkka. Literally everything is symbolism and exaggeration in this bombastic copy of the Sultan Ahmed Mosque in Istanbul, which was intended to underline the omnipotence of its builder, Muhammad Ali Pasha. But perhaps that is precisely what emphasizes by way of contrast the intimacy of the garlands of the 365 oil lamps (one for every day of the year, though they are today replaced by electricity) and nine chandeliers, which, in combination with small openings in the facade, provide light for its Prayer Hall.

The Industrial Revolution—which was already well underway when the Alabaster Mosque was constructed—revolutionized our worldview with its introduction of artificial light. This revolution is magnificently illustrated by another shining example Ilkka refers to: Van Gogh's *Café Terrace at Night*, which he painted in 1888, tellingly dividing his canvas into two equal parts. Gone here was the artist who, only three years earlier, had the figures in his *The Potato Eaters* gather round a dim oil-lamp, inspired by Rembrandt's *clair-obscur* or *chiaroscuro*. Instead, in *Terrace at Night* on the left he showed a café terrace illuminated by a single gas lamp, bathing in a sea of stark sulfurous yellow. Meanwhile on the right he painted—in accordance with Eugène Delacroix's rules regarding contrasting colors—the adjacent square and street with the starry sky above in countless shades of deep blue. As he wrote to his sister Wil, "I like finally getting rid of that conventional black night." To paint a starry sky, on the spot, at night, and outdoors, was the biggest obsession of the deeply religious Van Gogh in those days. The terrace provided him with the light he needed to become a pioneer with his depiction of the night sky in situ.

Familiar as most of us are now with the omnipresence of light, it is impossible to imagine what a dark place the world was back in the nineteenth century. Even after gas lighting became widespread in the 1850s, the brightest streetlamps still gave off less light than a modern twenty-five-watt bulb. So, it is very likely that the gas lamp on the terrace in Arles radiated only a faint glow, *The Avenue de Clichy: Five o'Clock in the Evening*, which his friend Louis Anquetin painted in Paris a year earlier, inspiring Van Gogh. But that was not the point. Less than ten years earlier, in 1879, Thomas Alvin Edison had patented the incandescent bulb and started a network of power-suppliers for electricity worldwide. In a little while, the world would actually look like Van Gogh's painting. By turning the pitch-black sky a majestic blue, he confirmed what Immanuel Kant already knew: that our experience of lightness is inherently subjective. The rest is Einstein & Son.

Scientists later concluded that the way Van Gogh shed light on the starry sky foreshadowed the two theories that Albert Einstein partly initiated from his analysis of the firmament, and which today determine our actions down to the smallest detail: the General Theory of Relativity and Quantum Mechanics. Even more, those theories—which were considered incompatible—become reconciled in the canvas. Up close one can see particles or *Quanta*, while from a distance a wave. Moreover, in one composition the greatest cosmic mystery, turbulence, was brought into clear focus.

Nearly a century and a half later, Suppanen, like the great contemporary light artists such as James Turrell and Olafur Eliasson, still handles the same cosmic perspective. Natural light and a starry sky rule, and artificial light plays a simple supporting role. Sometimes the light source is even missing, and the emphasis is instead placed on the way the object reflects and filters the surrounding light, such as in the glass objects that he creates with the glass blowers on the Venetian island of Murano. Glass is—as we all know—made from sand. And sand is the water of the desert. That can't be a coincidence either.

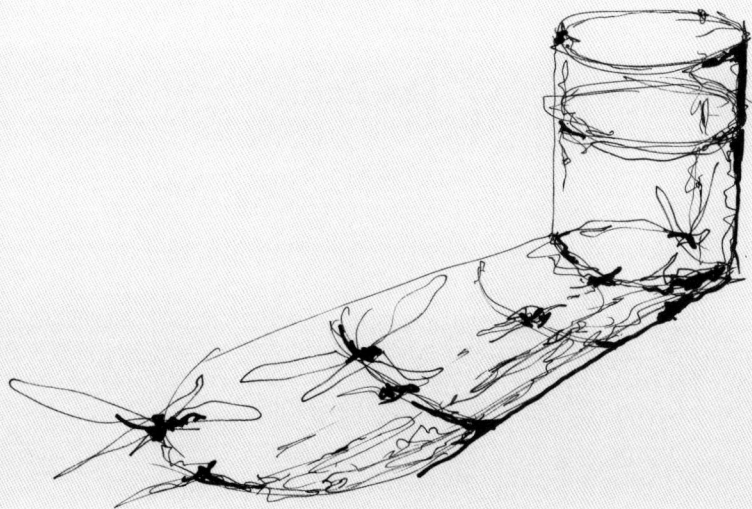

Fragility

04

Fragility represents a delicate balance between being deeply entrenched or transient, emerging from intentional or accidental circumstances. It carries with it dual implications of danger and hope—a precarity that questions whether situations will remain stable or change, flourish or break down. These moments are enveloped in a unique blend of poetic and rational lightness—the rational element coming from our inherent human desire for stability and understanding. Despite their uncertainty, these moments radiate a unique beauty and peace, and burst with potential. Consider for instance the moment the Berlin Wall came down in 1989, or the seeds of a dandelion.

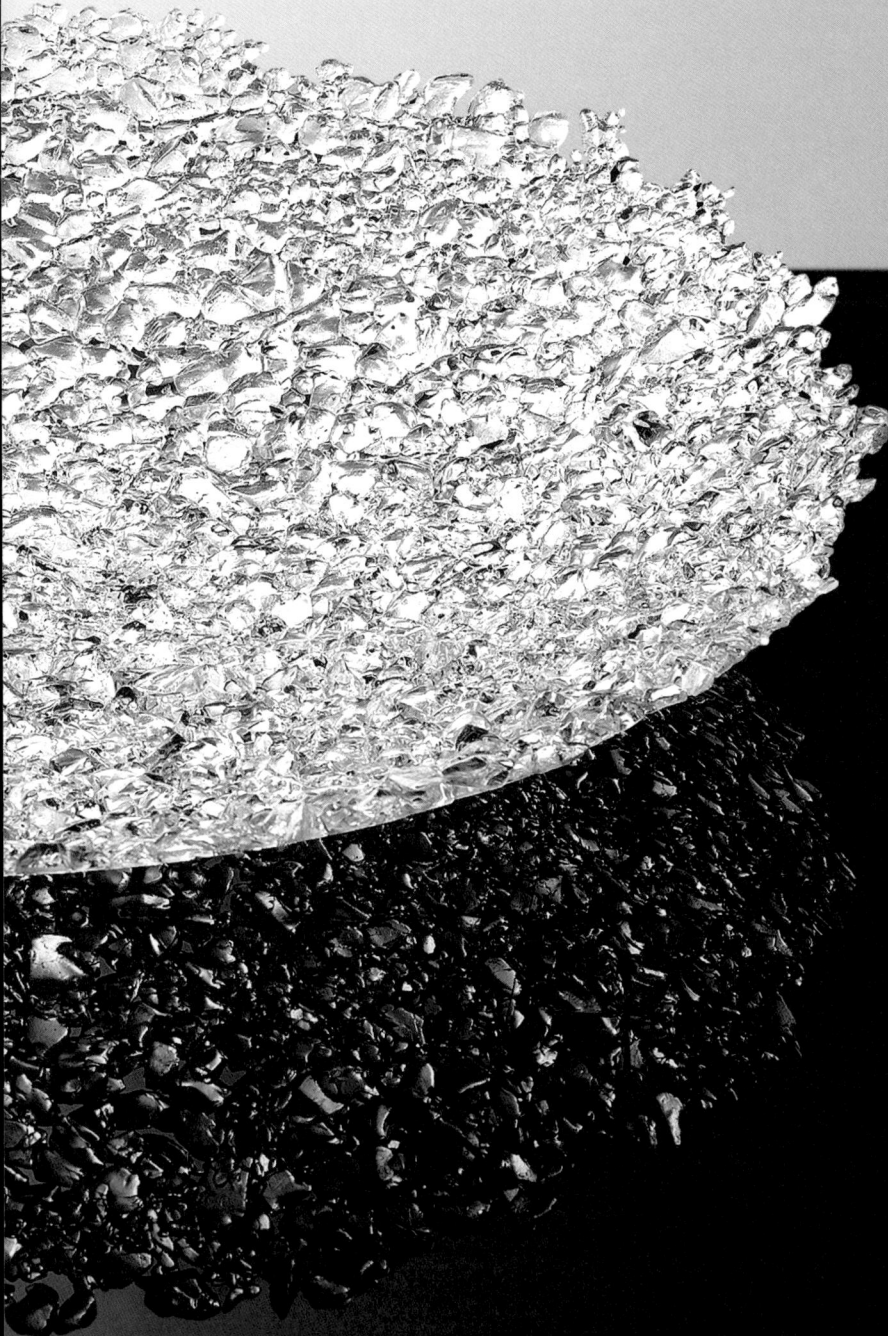

Broken & Dream

unique glass pieces,
Galerie Forsblom
2012

These two pieces represent the first time I really worked in glass. Previously I had only done industrial glass products for companies where my involvement was like a traditional designer, more or less delivering the drawings and then checking the samples before mass production. I began my work by visiting Murano, Venice, and talking to different glassmakers to see what they could do and how they did it. Soon I came across a technique whereby they melted pieces of glass together, and I felt an immediate understanding for its process and expression. It looked just like water freezing to ice, and then melting and freezing again into new shapes—a slow natural cycle I had observed all my life growing up in Finland. With the guidance of glass master Claudio Tiozzo, I learned from scratch by trial and error, making many different tests and gradually coming to the conclusion of what could be done. Broken consists of individual glass pieces in various sizes that then have been melted together in an oven. This is a process of heating and cooling that takes days. In one way it felt like baking a cake and the challenge was to understand the time and temperature to get the right effects in the glass. Dream consists of around 200 individually shaped glass pieces that are suspended in the air with thin threads. The finished result looks like ice that has melted in different ways, something which I am aware of I am not the first to achieve—it is no coincidence that my favorite glass series is Ultima Thule (1968) by the Finnish designer Tapio Wirkkala (1915–1985).

Brina
plate, Ercole Moretti
2010

This plate is made through a wonderful old technique in Murano called *murrina*, which is commonly used to make very decorative and colorful pieces. When you start to make something in glass, the glass is always in the shape of a ball. In this case you then apply layers of colored glass on top of the ball and, once your desired layers are there, somebody takes hold of a small piece of that ball and stretches it, and keeps stretching it until it becomes a several meters long glass rod. It is astonishing to see, and it is not always successful. All the different layers of glass are now in the shape of a one-centimeter-thick rod which are then cut up into preferred sizes like little pieces of candy. I decide how the pieces are placed in relation to each other and then they are melted together in a mold to form a whole piece. With the cooling down, polishing and sanding, this process takes weeks before you can actually see if what you wished for came true.

A wood log consists of large amounts of water. After it has been cut in the forest it is then dried, sometimes for years, before being used. If the wood is damp when used it will reform when it eventually dries and make an uneven and maybe undesired surface. In contrast, the craftsman Lorenzo Franceschinis, with whom I worked for this project, used wet wood on his wood lathe to shape an object after my design. This was then dried and later smeared and waxed with a metal coating. In this process the point is that nature takes over and the final shape is out of your control—which of course is difficult to accept as a designer. Nonetheless you embrace the unknown and that the wood may crack when it dries, in order to achieve a new expression. From the outset you are working with the possibility that you can fail, but you work with this rationally. If you reach a point where the object breaks, you recognize where this happens and adjust so it will not break on your next try. Experimentation by fact is like that, and it is perhaps the most important thing I can try to explain whenever I teach design at a university.

Coral
nesting bowls, unique piece
2019

Fireplace
Iittala
2008

I was brought in to help the Finnish company Iittala make a product range in a higher price segment. That kind of assignment usually means that you work conceptually before an actual design brief exists to try and understand in which direction to go. One concept which I continued to develop was related to fire. Getting a fireplace installed in your home is a considerable remodeling project, so the idea emerged to make a portable one, which also felt like a natural continuation of the company's history of making products for candles. During the course of this particular project, I became a pyrotechnic. We decided to use ethanol as fuel because it burns extremely well and then we lit it, and a still blue flame appeared. Staring at it in silence I realized that no one was ever going to pay to look at that. We had to understand how we could manipulate this flame to become yellow and moving and how this related to the burning process and air. The burning process could be regulated well enough through technique, however to make a flame move so it is pleasing to the eyes you have to create a certain disturbance in the air. This is hard to simulate in a model, so for the better part of a year we ran between rooms at the Iittala factory in Arabia, Finland, where there were different fires going on under various conditions. I designed a structure in stainless steel as a container for the liquid with a bent borosilicate glass frame around it. The glass frame was designed to make the air that circulates in the product semi-balanced. With equal distance from both openings, air reached the flame from two directions but not necessarily at the same time or with the same force and this created movement. When playing with fire you come to realize that there has always been a preferred natural size for making a fire across all cultures. People have gathered around a mid-sized fire through all ages, for warmth and cooking, and when the fire eventually turned into a TV it was more or less in the same size. So size was the one thing with which we did not need to experiment.

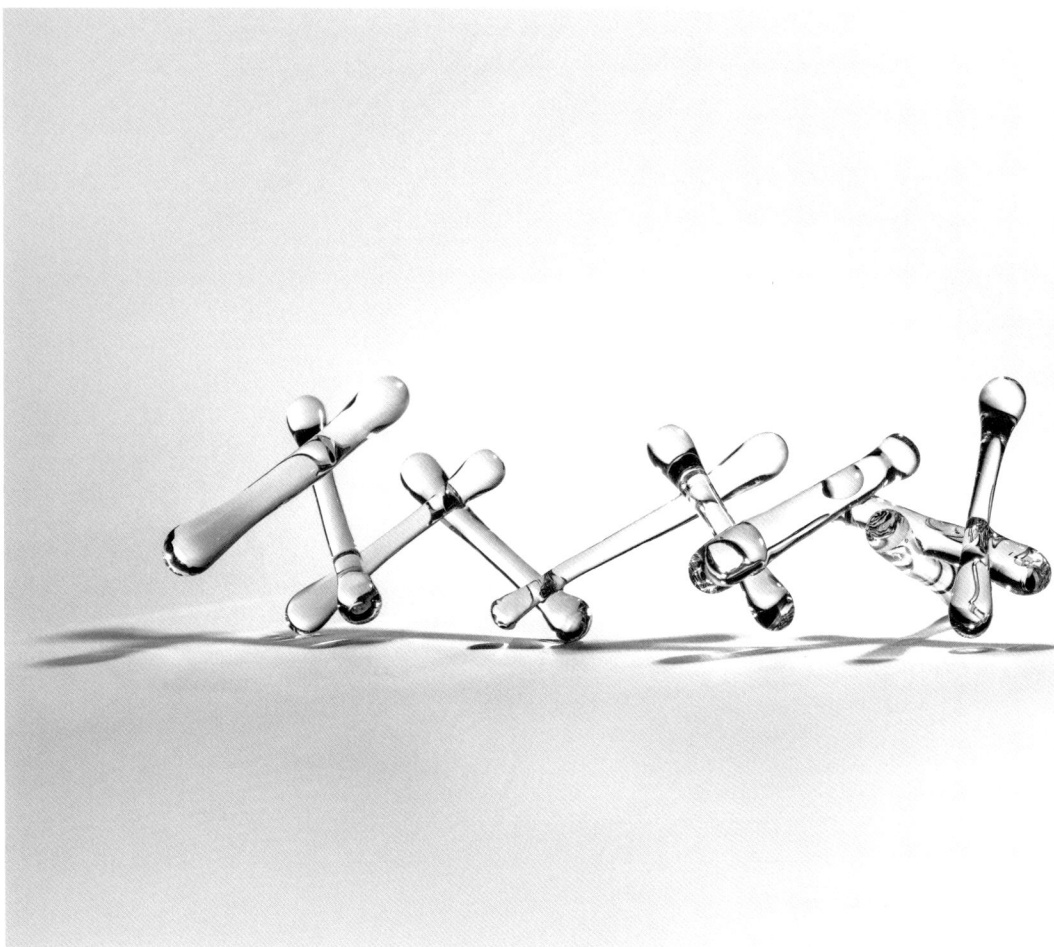

Experimental Piece

Ulrica Hydman Vallien Foundation
Kosta Boda
2024

I am self-taught when it comes to working in glass. I have learned by practice, by asking questions of skilled glass designers—who have all been very patient with me—and from studying glassmasters at work. The beginning for most glass pieces is a glass ball which you manipulate and build upon. In this case I departed from one component, which then is repeated and attached together to make a whole piece. In the world of handmade glass, this approach is a bit unusual and demands time for experimentation, time which I never really had. But when I received a prize from the Ulrica Hydman Vallien Foundation with the offer to work in the historic glassworks at Kosta in Sweden, I knew the time had come. I wondered how best to explain my idea to the glassmasters, and eventually made a scale model in wood to show them. The idea looked good in theory, but in reality, the technical challenge proved too overwhelming. It kept breaking down at the very last minute. This was mainly due to the heat, as all the pieces needed the exact right temperature to meld together. In the end we had to wait until all the components had cooled down and then glue them together, which was not the point. It felt like a defeat. Still, it looks both like it is defying gravity and as though it's very fragile—which it is. The fragility aspect contributes to making glass prestigious, because there is no way you can put it back together the same once it has broken. Each component in this structure is solid, with a little bit of air inside, which gives another set of reflections into the piece that makes it more alive. In the end I think we made a very good attempt. Experiments—ideas that did not work out as intended—hardly ever end up in books, because there is a sense of public shame among the stakeholders. But if you can get past the shame you can learn a lot by discussing them with others, therefore I think "mistakes" should be celebrated in the design world, rather than hidden. If I ever get the chance to try to do this structure again, I now know exactly what I would do differently to make it work.

The Unbearable Heaviness of Our Tangible Being

Leon Hidalgo

A fleeting moment, a precious wineglass and the wings of a firefly. A homeless person's makeshift shelter, an abandoned bridge and the spoked wheels of your bike. A reflected light flickering, a stranger's smile and a house of cards.

Fragility is part of our existence; it is drenched in risk and ephemerality, but also soaked with life. It is part of both the most beautiful and the worst moments we can remember. In a way, fragility and liveliness are parallel phenomena. When we experience joy, time passes faster. But it nevertheless passes, one way or the other, and decay becomes one of those persuasive representatives of the fragile.

Although human beings have become perfectionists in the illusion of permanence, fragility works precisely at the threshold between potential loss and the preciousness of existence itself. It is a reminder of the impermanent nature of things and, at the same time, an amplifier of their ephemeral beauty.

Nature is fragile. It is forever moving and growing, evolving and overcoming challenges magnificently. According to their expected life cycle, some plants grow fast and live short lives, while others grow slowly and live a long time. A tree can be seen as a metaphor for a fragility scale. Its trunk is massive, rooted tightly in the soil. This is the oldest part of the tree and thereby quite immovable and heavy. It grows slowly. On the other side of the scale, way up in the sky, we have its branches—light, fast-growing, and in constant motion. The leaf's life cycle is even smaller. You can almost watch them grow, collecting sunlight, turning yellow and brownish, then falling and decaying in the soil of the forest.

As humans, where do we put ourselves on this scale? Somewhere between lightness and heaviness; permanence and ephemerality; mobility and immobility?

The lighter an object, the easier it can be moved. If you order fragile glassware from overseas, it is packed in lightweight material, cardboard and foam. It is traveling on an airplane made from lightweight aluminum and composite materials before it arrives at your house. It says, "handle with care," which is great life advice, but also one of the main differences between fragility and lightness. Fragility requires maintenance

1="In biology material is expensive but shape is cheap. As of today, the opposite was true in the case of technology." See J. Vincent, "Biomimetic Patterns in Architectural Design," *Architectural Design* 79 (2009): 74–81.

2="Each German citizen accounts for about 480 tonnes of building materials." https://www.wernersobek.com/topics/the-future-of-construction/

and care. And while we inherently strive to care for things and people, this does bring with it the heaviness of worry and concern: a heaviness whose absence is the substance of feeling lightness in a philosophical sense.

In nature, shape is cheap, but material is expensive.[1] Dandelion seeds are designed to react to wind. They undock from the head of seeds to generate an uplift to travel great distances by air. The hair-like structure of the pappus serves as a parachute and as a tool to anchor in the ground for germination. The shapes that nature designs to address these challenges are incredibly complex—far more intricate than those constructed in our built environment.

The unbearable heaviness of our tangible being. The abundance of resources, just like the permanence of buildings, is an illusion feeding itself until it becomes overweight. The German engineer Werner Sobek is one of the people thinking about the actual weight of our built environment. He said that in Germany we have a weight of building resources of about 480 tons per person.[2] If we compare the weight of an ultralight outdoor tent like the Zpacks Duplex for two, made from highly durable Dyneema fiber weighing approximately 550g, with the substance of an average apartment in Berlin made from concrete weighing about 50t we find that the tent has a lifespan of approximately five to eight years, while an average building has fifty to eighty years. The lifespan of the building is around 100 times longer while weighing almost 100,000 times more than the tent. Settling down seemingly comes at an exponential gain in weight. But does it really?

The work of Russian engineer Vladimir Shukhov beautifully demonstrates how material scarcity can lead to innovative engineering. His towers and pipelines can be viewed as the skeletons of their heavyweight predecessors. The Shukhov Tower, consisting of six stacked grid shell hyperboloids, is as tall as a forty-story building. Completed in 1922, it was planned to be 15 meters higher than the Eiffel Tower (350m), while weighing less than a third of it. Changes during the process led to a constructed height of 150 meters with a staggeringly low weight of 240 tons. Although its appearance was fragile in the sense of "barely standing" it is indeed still standing after 100 years of defying the elements. A beauty of abandonment, or the emaciation of a monument.

Let's think about a bridge made of steel members. It is a skeleton of itself, dimensioned to persist. With time, the corrosion will begin to devour the material. We watch a time-lapse of decades wherein the components shrink and shrink until they are only a third of their original size. Barely standing, and there goes another millimeter taken by an ocean breeze of corrosive wind before, finally—it collapses. Broken. The state of fragility is gone and with it the beauty of its most bare existence.

Resilience

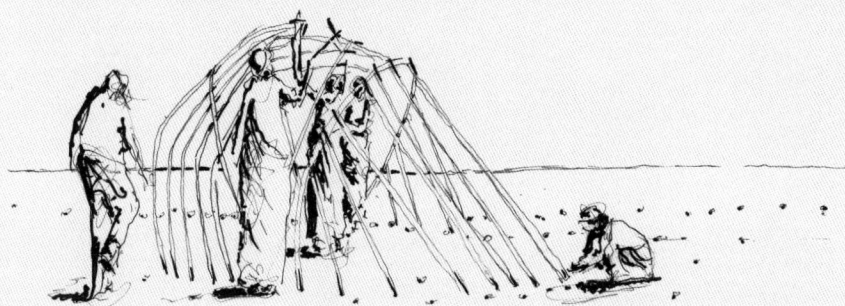

05

"Resilience" can be defined as the capacity to maintain a positive outlook in the face of adversity. To remain competent enough to navigate through a tough situation without being ensnared by past disappointments or failures. This translates into a "lightness of thought." A mindset that prompts us to use every available resource, no matter how small or seemingly insignificant, and transform these into meaningful actions to achieve our desired goals. This process is less about the grandeur of the resources and more about the resourcefulness of the individual. Examples include unplanned urban settlements such as the Favelas in Rio de Janeiro, or the Italian Arte Povera movement of the 1960s.

Trash left out on the street in a Brazilian city is most likely picked up by a *catadore*, a person who collects waste. Some catadores organize themselves in co-operatives that are situated under bridges to keep their findings dry from rain. Here they gather to separate metal from plastics, colored glass from clear glass and so forth. They might even have a machine that compresses cardboard boxes into manageable cubes. This waste is later sold to and collected by the official recycling plants. Most of the catadores are without a permanent address and the bottom line is that they work like entrepreneurs in recycling in order to survive. I was invited to one such co-op in the city of São Paulo, and went with the belief that I could help them change their situation for the better. After spending some time there, it was clear that they needed signage because a lot of people who drove by to dump their waste left hazardous objects like old batteries. Clear signs would instantly explain what the co-op could and could not handle. E-waste is very profitable for catadores, but to open up a computer and remove the precious metals with your bare hands is hard work, so we supplied them with the right tools. This whole experience left me with two insights. Firstly, that as a designer of physical products it is important to acknowledge—in a naive way—that you are also designing waste. Therefore, to see up close what kind of things end up as waste by default and by practice, and what kind of things are kept, is very sobering. The second insight was that traditional forms of designing physical products were of no use here. This is something that has continued to bother me. I could not really make a difference for these people with the skillset I had. I felt lost, and when I realized that these co-ops will eventually be pushed out by big business, since waste management and recycling will dominate the future, I felt even worse. I call them the "angels of São Paulo" because they work like angels, invisible to the society while nevertheless making it better.

Angels of São Paulo
consulting
2012

This project was initiated by a Finnish non-governmental organization (NGO) who support the livelihood of women without caste in rural India. People without a caste are also without rights in their society and risk abuse in any enterprise, which makes the involvement of NGOs so important. I got to work in a village where they had a tradition of weaving bamboo baskets, and the aim here was to find ways to secure work which would generate fairer and increased earnings for them. By turning the baskets upside down, they could enter a new typology as lampshades and be sold at a higher price. In addition to this reconfiguration I also drew a collection of different shades. The collection of handmade lamps was successfully launched, however it did not take long before the style became a trend and large chains presented a similar range for one tenth of our price, which basically killed the opportunity for us. Our operations were in no way equipped to adapt to the fast-changing trends of the market—too late I realized I should have gained more understanding of the complexity of the situation at the beginning. While we did not succeed on the scale at which we had hoped to, or find a sustainable solution for the production, it was an attempt and for that it needs to be acknowledged. As a designer I am always optimistic and at the bare minimum it is always better to have tried than not. But this made me reflect on the very idea, or expectations, of the designer as someone who enters the scene and solves all problems. A lingering image from the twentieth century when architects and designers were able to realize their visions on grand scales in the ruins after the world wars. What will be the image in the twentieth-first century I wonder?

Tikau
light collection
2011

On Resilience

Maria Cecilia Loschiavo dos Santos

Across the world, social exclusion has created a landscape of poverty in which certain survival practices and tactics become necessary and prevalent amongst the population. In Brazil, one example of this phenomenon is the urban practice of recycling, which is represented by the *catadores*—waste pickers—who are a common presence in its cities. They emerge from extreme poverty to become resourceful workers who are well adapted to the market. Moreover they also function like civil servants; careful citizen responsible for the promotion of a sustainable urban environment. Although they have been visible on the streets of Brazilian cities for several decades, it was not until the beginning of the 1980s that the first initiatives arose to organize the catadores through associations or cooperatives. For instance, in São Paulo a group of church-workers—led by the nuns Irmã Dalva Ivete de Jesus and Regina Maria Manoel—started helping homeless people who began collecting and selling waste that had been discarded by homes, industries and commercial establishments in the downtown area.

It is important that this phenomenon is not understood in terms of pity or commiseration, but rather through the lens of political consciousness and community organizing. With a broad knowledge of materials and their urban life-cycle, these activists have created a new economy with a significant focus upon the valorization of waste materials and their relevance to the environment, while also exposing the astonishing level of economic inequality in Brazil. Brazil has indeed fostered several innovative policies that promote inclusive recycling, including by legally recognizing the role of waste picker cooperatives and integrating them into the formal waste system. But despite the importance of their work and the complex operations and services delivered by catadores, their livelihood has not improved to the extent hoped.

Environmental issues are at the center of contemporary debates. As the Argentinian painter, theorist and designer Tomás Maldonado (1922–2018) wrote in his preface to a book on Italian industrial designer Medardo Chiapponi, the environment "is the question of questions."[1] The environment magnetizes an extraordinary variety of urgent conflicts that each require solutions and cry out for policies, since our life on Earth depends on them.

1=Tomás Maldonado, "Presentazione," in Medardo Chiapponi, *Ambiente, gestione e strategia, Un contributo alla teoria della progettazione ambientale,* Milano, 1989.

2=Carl Sagan, *Pale Blue Dot: A Vision of the Human Future*, New York/London, 1994.

3=Maria Cecilia Loschiavo dos Santos, "Cities of Plastic and Cardboard, The informal Cities Habitat of home-less people in São Paulo, Los Angeles and Tokyo", professorship thesis, University of São Paulo, 2003.

As the American astronomer Carl Sagan (1934–1996) argued, "we need to preserve and cherish that pale blue dot, the only home we've ever known."[2] In a time of excess, over-production and hyper-consumption, the production of waste is growing nonstop. On a humid afternoon in the city of São Paulo, the catadore Carlos Roberto Fabrício exclaimed in an interview "It is incredible, I collect one cartload a day, and I ask myself, where does so much trash come from? It seems endless. It makes me sad to see a huge quantity of trash, especially food, thrown away."[3] It is the waste pickers who have presented a solution that breaks with the traditional attitudes towards trash, and call on us all to rethink the problem. They have well understood, under the pressure of their circumstances, that what has been castoff can come back around.

The perception of the waste picker's work and culture by the Brazilian public occupies a spectrum between sympathetic humanitarian impulses and feelings of repulsion and indignation. But it is a clear fact that their practices have had positive effects. From the physical perspective they extend the life of materials and products, and they reduce waste. Their contribution goes beyond this, however. Under the pressure of adaptation to survive in a hostile environment, the waste picker's work is integral to the very metabolism of the city and the preservation of the planet itself.

Their collective efforts and struggle eventually culminated in the organization of a social movement, the *Movimento Nacional de Catadores de Materiais Recicláveis*. In June 2001, the First National Conference of Paper and Recyclable Materials Collectors took place on the campus of the National University of Brasília. This gathering marked the official creation of a national movement with the participation of more than 1700 collectors from all over Brazil. They arrived in crowded buses to collaborate on writing a political agenda articulating and advocating their rights, as well as establishing partnerships with different sectors of civil society. Later this resulted in a network in Brazil and Latin America, the "Recyclable Material Collectors Latin American Network," based on the principles of solidarity. In December 2010, as a testament to their power as a national movement, they managed to organize and host *Natal na Rua* (Christmas on the Street), an event attended by the outgoing and the incoming President of Brazil, Luiz Inácio Lula da Silva and Dilma Rousseff, respectively. This was not simply a Christmas photo opportunity, but a public accountability action in which the ruling Worker's Party signed several initiatives that incorporated the demands of the waste picker organizations before thousands of their members.

The catadores of Brazil have shown to society at large that although their individual lives are permeated by vulnerability and precarity, their collective efforts and sheer resilience can affect political power and build social movements that inspire a contagious solidarity.

Structures

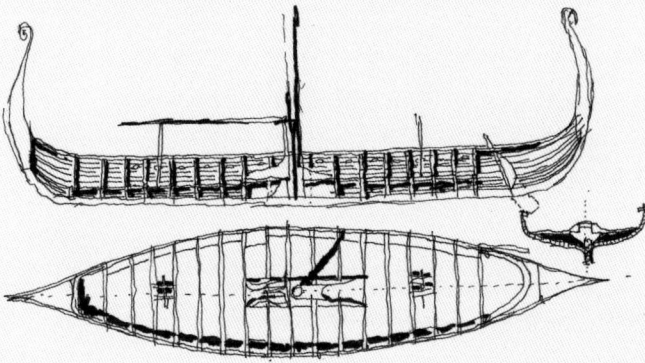

06

Light structures are essential in our quest for efficiency. The market is moving in favor of larger objects—bigger cars, sprawling condominiums and jumbo jetliners. This is a trajectory that challenges us to grapple with the dual difficulties of escalating costs associated with energy conversion for production, distribution and waste disposal, along with the dwindling availability of raw materials. An equation that demands not just lighter but also smarter structures. In austere conditions with minimal resources the structure we build is reduced to its bare minimum. Here, the visible structure itself becomes the form and transforms into an expressive representation of the forces that are fundamental to its creation. As clearly seen in the traditional fishing machine referred to as a *travoc* along the Adriatic Coast of Abruzzo, or the structure of a wooden ship.

Like a building, a table has to not only withstand gravity but also sideway forces, since people constantly bump into tables or lean on them. And while we need a table to be very strong, we also need to consider using as little material as possible for its structure. In this case we achieved it by using a very thin metal bar to construct the legs. One single bar is moving in a complex line, overlapping itself from left to right like a knot, creating diagonals. This results in a barely detectable asymmetric expression, which simultaneously serves another purpose. To make the table more rigid, the steel bar has to be welded in places, and even if this is done with precision by computer-aided machinery, it might still be visible—which is annoying from an aesthetic point of view. But in Litta the metal is bent in such way that the welding is always under the bar and therefore hidden from our eyes.

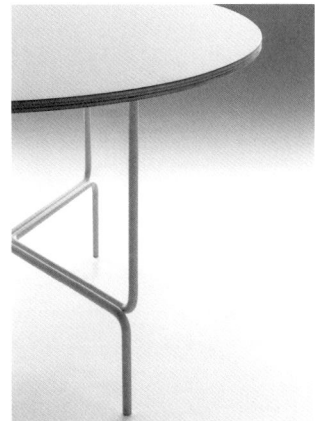

Litta
tables, with Raffaella Mangiarotti, Manerba 2019

In Nordic countries it is common to have a "summer house," which is a kind of ideal living condition in the middle of the nature, used from around May until October. Many people prefer this over anything else, and here they accept fewer conveniences than in their daily life in the city. This summer house is situated on a hill on an island in the Finnish archipelago, and it was designed after studying two phenomena closely—the sun and the wind. Up north we like to get the sun into our homes at the right moments: in the morning and in the evening when the sun sets—during Midsummer this happens around 11 p.m. Therefore, the openings and windows were designed in such way that the sun rises at the breakfast table, with some shadow during the day, and in the evening lights up and catches the last rays of the sun. While the sun is predictable, you have to observe the wind to anticipate it and then build accordingly to get the most leeward. This wooden house was built by two people, a father and son. It meant that when I designed the house, I had to calculate the maximum weight of each and every piece so they would be able to carry it from their boat, up the hill and to the site, with the exception of the large windows. This is more or less a self-sufficient building. There is no running water, and enough electricity is generated through solar panels on the roof to power a television, stereo and lamps. There is also a gas stove. The number of trees that dies annually on the island—which is about one or two—gives enough wood for the open fire to warm up the house and a sauna.

Villa Ilo
private house
2004

This sauna is located not far from the main house, on a flat terrain, and close to the water, since part of the experience is to be able to cool down quickly. On the small porch, wooden lathes function as sunscreen as well as protection from the wind. The lathes slow the wind down in a pleasant way, while a solid wall would have created wind turbulence. Like some Japanese temples, this building has a light structure and an open, rectangular space within, in which you move "diagonally," from corner to corner. Traditionally, a sauna is divided into a room with a heater, washing room and dressing room. And even though it is a small unit, it is essential in Finnish architecture and therefore normally is built first in housing developments. The main reason, that it serves the basic needs for heat and hygiene, which can be lifesaving at times. For instance, my grandmother who lived out in the countryside far away from any hospital therefore had to give birth to my mother in the sauna.

Sauna Ilo
2004

Helsinki Contemporary
private gallery
2005

Most often you find art in galleries lit up by spotlights facing the wall, but there are artists who find an "even" light more desirable for their work. We therefore had two parallel lighting systems installed in this gallery, tracks with spotlights and fluorescent light tubes in the ceiling. To enhance the effect, we had not only the walls but also the floor painted white, so that light could reflect from as much surface as possible. This creates an unusual condition where all shadows are eliminated in the room, which is ideal for paintings, but not preferable for three-dimensional objects since shadows are how we experience the shape of things. To complement the white surfaces in the space we left some areas in their original raw state, like concrete pillars, brick walls, and some beautifully made ventilation tubes. This created an interesting contrast in materiality, a dialogue between rough and refined space—actually, it turned out that most artists wanted to hang their best piece on the brick wall. A staircase to the upper floor and a reception desk was made in steel and a couple of small tables were made in untreated copper. And all the wine that has been spilt during the openings has slowly given these tables a wonderful patina. In the home of the gallery owner there is a stair rail in the shape of a snake. I thought to myself "this snake needs an apple," and decided to turn the door handle at the entrance to the gallery in to one. This did not require any design. I chose the best-looking apple at the supermarket and then had it cast in bronze as it was. In fact, the door handle might be the only part of the architecture that you are allowed to touch in a gallery, and with time this apple looked great through oxidation and the combined touch of all the art lovers.

Fire Pit
Finnish Pavilion
Shanghai World Fair
2010

The Finnish architectural firm JKMM designed a circle-shaped pavilion, almost like a bowl. Walking inside it along a path you eventually reached its heart, an open-air inner courtyard. Since the beginning of time most buildings have been erected around a fire. And although the design of this pavilion was truly contemporary, it nevertheless called for a traditional fireplace. My design involved opening a four-meter-wide immersed circle in the floor of the courtyard, which could also be covered up. I then designed a firepit in the middle of the circle, so people could gather around it, effectively creating a sense of intimacy in this vast space.

Art Cross

space divider, Vivero
2019

This is a light, foldable and freestanding unit that defines different areas within the same open space, while fulfilling the need for privacy. Two different kinds of screens can be used with it, either a fireproof and printable paper, or an acoustic felt material made of wool and recycled plastic. The thin metal frame is composed of diagonals to make it rigid—in theory you have to create a diagonal in a structure for stability. The structure of an object is most often hidden behind a shell of some sort, but in Art Cross it is visible. I love the idea of making a structure visible, because then anybody can get an idea of how things work. Just look at the façades in gothic architecture, where gravity is so clearly expressed, such as the Duomo in Milan. Or the façades of the Centre Pompidou in Paris, which immediately makes you understand how the building breaths.

This company was founded in 1954, and from its studio in the Flatiron District in Manhattan, New York, it for many years made lifelike mannequins for shopping windows facing the big avenues. This has always been a job for a sculptor, and today all the furniture that they create in their studio is still made by the hand of a sculptor. Digital renderings were of no use here. I made my drawings on paper in a one-to-one scale, because that is how a sculptor works, they understand 2D perfectly in 3D. The lines were gradually transferred from the paper into an object in plaster, and then finally molded. Being around such knowledge and skill, talking about design in the same refined way as art, in such a wonderful setting as a sculptor's studio, was simply wonderful and the whole experience brought me back to my art classes in school many years ago.

In parts, this collection derives from two historic examples, which always have fascinated me. The Spanish architect Antoni Gaudí (1852–1926) had a certain way of making models for his buildings. He used weights or gravity to stretch strings that he tied together in sequence and levels. Then, looking at the cluster of strings upside down, he could study the shape of his building, knowing that the opposite forces at the ends of each string had perfect compression and therefore optimal arches. The roof of the SC Johnson Administration Building (1939) in Racine, Wisconsin, USA, designed by the American architect Frank Lloyd Wright (1867–1959), is upheld by columns that expand like trumpets. Beside the beauty of this shape, it leaves a minimal footprint on the floor while it withstands a lot of pressure from above. With this in mind I stretched stockings through holes in a cardboard box, and pinned them to the bottom to achieve conical columns of my own. I then used my model as an efficient and aesthetically pleasing structure to build my furniture. I really enjoy shapes that are made in this way, as opposed to shapes that are made as a result of some inner desire.

Furniture Collection
Ralph Pucci International
2025

Lightness

———

Toshiko Mori

On the surface, the sensation of "lightness" inspires good feelings, conjuring the dream of being freed from gravity. But in today's context, lightness has become a loaded word. It is heavy with implication because we cannot simply isolate an effect without first contextualizing it. Lightness as an idea perhaps had more of an uplifting and optimistic nuance in the recent past, but in our time, what does it mean to be "light" without being "lite," or devoid of frivolity? What inspires anew our desire for "lightness"? While we live in a complex, conflict-ridden world full of crises—climatic, societal, economic and political—we may find that lightness radiates a beacon to guide us forward.

The term's interconnectedness with weight, perception and material-use directly resonates with our collective anxiety about shouldering burdens; the results of our desire to live lightly translates to a false sense of comfort, luxury and manufactured ideas of efficiency and ease. This impression of lightness is often hiding something heavier and more burdensome, eschewing critical understanding in favor of quick illusions. In architecture and in culture generally, these "lite" constructions obscure the demand for innovation or invention necessary for solutions to the myriad crises we face.

Metaphysically speaking, if we were to become open to a future which embraces diverse perspectives and cultures, we would need to unload the weight of historically constructed prejudices and preconceptions. We need to be mentally light, agile and emotionally open to empathy, instead of leaning on resistance and unwillingness to change. Lightness in our outlook on the future results in a generous attitude, encourages kindness to others and relieves anger and hate.

Physically speaking, we need to lighten structural loads to save ourselves from various earthly disasters. The art of building in the future should rely more on subtraction than addition. Buildings must urgently shed weight to improve their resilience against earthquakes and hurricanes. To make existing buildings seismically resistant, one can reduce weight by lessening deadloads and using this extra capacity to add elements that bolster against ever increasing lateral forces, such as hurricane-force winds or earthquakes. Buildings also need to become more flexible; instead of being designed to work against the forces of nature, we ought to transform buildings to work with these forces, designing them to yield and accept rather than pursuing engrained strategies of constant resistance. By allowing movement in design, choreographing this movement, enabling structures to translate forces through materials, understanding the degree and duration of impact and enabling them to release these forces, a change to our conception of structure begins to emerge, as a means of working with dynamic forces rather than static weights. Lightness of structure introduces yielding as a positive attribute and an alternative to the constant addition of weight to continuously bolster mass.

One book that I reference constantly on this subject is *Lightness: The Inevitable Renaissance of Minimum Energy Structures*, edited by Adriaan Beukers and Ed van Hinte and published in Rotterdam in 1998. In it, the authors look at "lightness" from the perspective of materials, shapes and processes. Beukers and van Hinte cite examples of not only the direct effect of lightness in materials and structures, but also discuss indirect effects which can play an exponential role in infrastructure, not just roads and airports but also energy and water networks. This book also points out the essential quality of efficiency in many different forms to govern logistics, distribution systems, and transportation, which can in turn diffuse lightness across all aspects of economy and environment.

In my opinion, having a light carbon footprint is the most impactful expression of lightness for our time. It is also a necessity if we wish to survive the climate crisis. The embodied energy of materials is a huge component in the calculation of this footprint, and we must think about where our materials come from, how they are sourced or transported, and how, where, and by whom they are fabricated. It is also imperative to think about material circularity, both in terms of material lifecycle and its afterlife as the reuse and recycling of objects and buildings. Further, the operation of buildings and their designed elements are continuous sources of energy consumption. Lightness in this context translates to passive design, orienting projects to enhance optimal performance without an over-reliance on mechanical means. The battle against climate change begins by reimagining how lightly we can live and exist, so that our dependence on heavily engineered artificial climates can be minimized. Behavioral change, rather than any technological innovation, can have the most significant impact on our carbon footprints. If we dress lightly in warm seasons, we can tolerate the heat, and if we layer ourselves in cold seasons, winter spaces do not require excess heating. We must learn to become lighter and more tolerant, mobile, creative and open; we should opt to walk and bike instead of getting into a car, to eat more organic produce instead of consuming industrialized agricultural and disposable products.

A light touch will show that we do not need excess equipment to operate buildings, and will instead lead us to think about how lightly we can inhabit spaces and embrace natural forces to enhance our lives. The character of a new kind of luxury is the ability to live closer in alignment with nature. This begs us to question consumer culture, especially in the design of objects, furniture, and lighting fixtures which build in functional and aesthetic obsolescence to promote further unnecessary production. Do we need more new chairs and new products; can we diminish our material possessions? Is there a way to live with less? Is there a way to share what we have with others to reduce waste in material culture?

Lightness has the potential to be the greatest game changer in the battle against the climate crisis because it can turn wasteful behavior into efficient, economical and thoughtful solutions that can be implemented across multiple scales. Lightness is not just an adjective for the objects and buildings we create. Rather than constantly struggling against accumulated habits and notions of comfort, lightness in our time also means a return to living in harmony with nature, and with each other, by shedding the unnecessary weight of matters and materials.

Philosophically, lightness is frequently linked to the concept of freedom, stemming from an existence unencumbered by the burdens of physical or psychological constraints. This is an idea that also occurs through literature, where lightness often signifies a tone of hope and optimism. This metaphysical lightness can be interpreted as a liberation from fear and an embrace of the potential for radical shifts in thought, veering away from the entrenched perspectives of the past. It encourages the unlearning of ingrained knowledge, making room for the creation and the exploration of new thoughts, ideas, or movements. Without such a lightness, there could have been no punk or civil rights movement.

I am Finnish, I sit in my home on Alvar Aalto furniture, I studied architecture at the Alvar Aalto University in Otaniemi, and when I meet someone outside of Finland, I am often questioned about Alvar Aalto. So, when I was preparing an exhibition of my work in Maison Louis Carré (1959), a beautiful building by Alvar Aalto in the south of Paris, it was not completely uncomplicated for me. Frankly it gets "too much" sometimes, and I find myself thinking that it would almost be simpler if there was no Alvar Aalto, since as a Finnish designer your work will always be seen in relation to his. Therefore, I felt compelled to undertake a piece that would both address this feeling and at the same time show my admiration for the Japanese designer Shiro Kuramata (1934–1991). In 1985 Kuramata created his *Homage to Josef Hoffmann*, during which he wrapped a wooden chair in metal wires and burned it, and that is the technique I borrowed. I welded metal sticks around Aalto's famous wooden stool E60 (1934) and set it ablaze. This sooty metal skeleton was then anodized and included in the exhibition, and I like it in many ways, although I am not sure what it means in the end. This was not an act of aggression; it was simply a reaction to an overwhelming feeling. It is "Burning Aalto," which I have every right to do. In a way I had to do it, like an angry teenager rebelling against his father to show that he is a person in his own right.

Burning Aalto
unique piece, Galerie
Maria Wettergren
2017

Anniversary
coin series
2017

The Finnish government asked several designers to propose anniversary coins to celebrate 100 years of Finnish independence. A series of five coins, each coin representing two decades of Finnish history. The concept I proposed was simple. On one side of the coin, you show the achievement of a nation in that period of time, and on the other side a challenge in that same period. I decided to use architecture as representation of the societal achievements and made a selection of five buildings together with a professor of Finnish architecture. I then went through and tried to identify the biggest challenges in these five centuries with another professor, and finally proceeded to design the coins. A coin is a very small object in which you barely see what is illustrated on it. But when these coins were presented in the media, they were enlarged and featured together with the historical photographs I had used in the design process. The first coin to be released in the series illustrated the brutal and deadly Finnish Civil War. Next to this photograph it read that it was in celebration of Finland's independence. This immediate combination could naturally be interpreted as if we had meant to celebrate our independence by showing a moment in history when Finns turned in rage against each other— and that is exactly how it was interpreted. There was an uproar, and some dramatic hours in my life followed.

I remember being in a meeting at a hotel in Helsinki that morning. I had my phone on silent mode and when I gave it a glance halfway through, I saw that I had 272 missed calls. That was a surprise, so when the meeting finished, I hurried out to get back to my office. But out on the street a black van suddenly drove up and blocked the way to my car. The side doors flung open, and a person started filming me, I had no idea what was going on and I froze. After five seconds the door closed, and the van drove off. I managed to get a glimpse of the car plates, which read "CD," which meant that it was a diplomatic car. Most likely a neighbor in the east who wanted to know who I was, but the fact that they had known where I would be that morning made my mind race in all directions.

It seemed that every single person in Finland had an opinion about my coins, and they were mostly negative. It was the main news on all the news channels, "Was it is really true that this guy wanted to celebrate

Finland by showing Finnish people killing each other!?"
Even politicians, regardless of their political views,
were upset. Coins such as these are official money,
which means that the Ministry of Finance has to sign
off on them, which they had done. But that afternoon
the political pressure became too much and forced the
Minister of Finance to publicly issue a statement saying
that the coins I had designed were to be withdrawn. At
my office I opened my inbox and saw a large amount
of hate mail from people who thought that I should be
shot like the people on the coin. There was just no way I
could begin to explain myself, to try and convince some
stranger that they had not understood my intention. It is
a strange thing to be inside a public storm such as this,
because on the inside it is very quiet, it was just me,
alone in front of my desk.

      I still think this was a good project with a valid
idea. In 1918 Finland went through a gruesome Civil
War that lasted about five and a half months and during
which around 40,000 people were killed. Its daily kill
ratio is still one of the highest in the world, of any civil
war. For me, the principal idea of this coin series was
that everything has another side. Finland is independent
and we are a wonderful country, but it is also a historical
fact that once we were animals to each other. Through
it all I never thought that this scandal was about me, but
rather about this painful memory which is a part of our
collective identity in Finland.

      Some time later the National Museum of
Finland asked if they could borrow the drawings for the
coins to be exhibited, which of course i was happy to do.
But not long after they had picked up the drawings at my
studio, I received a message saying that the Ministry of
Finance had come to the museum and confiscated them.
This all felt rather staged, as if they just wanted to get
rid of them, and honestly, I did not care, because what
I had given them were copies of the originals. For some
time, I felt people were a bit scared of confronting me,
scared of having anything to do with someone who had
just been publicly prosecuted, and it sort of affected
my work in Finland, or at least the possibility of getting
new clients for a while. But I do not blame them, and
I sincerely feel that as an outcome of this, I became a
stronger person than I had been before.

The Finnish word *Kivikko* roughly translates to "rocky ground" and that was an image I had in my mind, which I wanted to translate into a form of alternative comfort—a seating system in the spirit of the radical designs of the late 1960s and 70s. I was designing some textiles for the Finnish company Marimekko, known for their strong and colorful patterns on fabrics and clothes, and every time I came to check on the progress I brought them new ideas. When I showed them the sketches for Kivikko, they immediately jumped on it and were adventurous enough to make it into a product. Kivikko consists of five different sized balls, where the largest is over one meter in diameter and the smallest the size of a football. Instead of hiding the seams as is traditionally done with clothes I reversed it so that they are visible. And when the series are together, they make sense in a fun, relaxed way, which kids are the first to figure out, turning them into castles and mountains in no time.

Kivikko
seating furniture,
Marimekko
2009

Don't Forget to Play

exhibition architecture,
ArkDes – the Swedish Center for
Architecture and Design
2008

The museum of architecture in Stockholm, Sweden, asked if I could design an exhibition about Alvar Aalto furniture. I am aware it sounds arrogant, but this might be the most lifeless assignment you can get as a Finnish architect or designer, and I had to motivate myself to develop an interesting concept that went beyond merely praising the beauty of these furniture. Alvar Aalto once said "don't forget to play" and that is what I wanted to do, make the exhibition more into an event of continuous change instead of something traditional and static. All the furniture was white at the opening, but over the course of the exhibition, groups of children were invited to unleash their creativity on them with finger paint, gradually transforming them into something wild and colourful. The exhibition architecture consisted of wooden sticks hanging from the ceiling. which gave an atmosphere of a forest, while also creating a negative space for visitors to move around in and see these new classics.

On Lightness of Thought

Ilkka Suppanen

Writing and speaking about lightness often evokes a sense of freedom—a state of existence that transcends the limits of bodily, emotional, social and existential constraints. Lightness immediately contrasts with heaviness, which represent responsibility for making concrete decisions that have irreversible consequences in the material world. The term "heaviness" is also used to characterize the processes of inheritance, traditionalism, the solidification of free movement and the reification of ideas into facts. It is associated with the demands of ethical responsibility and the weight of moral and existential choices. So, lightness and heaviness both have crucial, important places in human experience. When thinking becomes too rigid or burdened by the heaviness of established norms and rules, it can stifle both creativity and the capacity of adaptation.

Milan Kundera's novel *The Unbearable Lightness of Being* (1984) explores this existential duality. To begin with, it suggests that lightness always seems desirable, as it implies freedom from responsibility and life in deliverance. However, the novel also argues that if the lightness of thought and action is not supported by any deeper engagement with the world, then it can become directionless or meaningless, and ultimately grow empty. Thus understood, lightness can easily be used as a metaphor for liberation— freedom from the heaviness of societal norms and pressures, and even the demands of existence itself. It also represents the openness that one feels when liberated from the internal constraints of guilt, fear, vanity and shame. This symbolic function is cross-cultural, perhaps even universal, since mental and emotional burdens weigh heavily on us all, limiting our abilities to act, express and communicate with the world. Therefore, lightness can be interpreted as liberation from fear and as an embrace of our human potential for radical shifts in thinking, veering away from the entrenched perspectives of the past.

The Punk movement, which emerged in the 1970s, is usually associated with rebellion, resistance to authority and a do-it-yourself (DIY) attitude that rejects mainstream measures and conventions. At first glance, the movement may appear to be motivated by certain forms of heaviness— anger, defiance and confrontation with societal norms. However, when examined more closely, Punk can be seen as a powerful expression of freedom, adaptability, the rejection of bigotry and the weight of oppressive forces. Punk embodies a form of lightness that embraces spontaneity, experimentation and creative liberation, unburdened by social expectations and rigid systems of thought. At its core, Punk was about rejecting the "heaviness" of all established structures, not only political institutions and societal expectations, but also the corporate influence on art and music and traditional measures of excellence that the arts themselves recapitulate. The labels of rebellion and resistance—two words that evoke mental images of serious, societal implications—are usually attached to Punk and hinder us from seeing the inner lightness of this movement and the joy of creativity and experimentation that it offers. The lightness of do-it-yourself is reflected in the movement's rejection of the rigidity of established frameworks of production. It allows—and also requires—an openness to experimentation, a playfulness with identities and a continual reinvention of the world. This is not any infantile outburst but a reinvention of the idea of autonomy characteristic of enlightenment.

We often underestimate the impact of lightness on thoughts and actions. Symbolically understood, both heaviness and lightness are essential aspects of the human experience and can therefore be found across influential movements, thoughts and texts. On August 28, 1963, Dr. Martin Luther King Jr. delivered his famous "I Have a Dream" speech, during the March on Washington for Jobs and Freedom. MLK's address is widely regarded as one of the most significant speeches in the history of late modernity, particularly for its powerful message on equality. His speech became a global symbol of nonviolence and hope. Even though many people may not have heard or read the entire speech, its influence remains profound and far-reaching for several reasons. It remains important, first, because its message transcends time and location. The call for equality, justice and freedom resonates not only with the North American struggle for civil rights and liberties, but also with universal human rights movements around the world. Yet more importantly, MLK's speech also expresses the idea of lightness in its forward-looking attitude. It emphasizes the importance of letting go of the heavy burdens of the past, however weighty they may be—loaded as they are with racism, oppression, rightful anger and hatred.

While recollecting the heaviness of the sufferings of segregation and police brutality, the speech promotes freedom, hope and collectivity—which all reflect and emanate the light of a new liberated condition of co-existence.

MLK's speech offers a message of hope that inspires and encourages subjects to believe in the possibility of a more just world. It contains both the heaviness of demands for ethical responsibility and the lightness of hope. Optimism, as a component of such lightness, empowers all King's audiences, past and present, and encourages them to rise above the weight of their circumstances and to envision a future in which justice and equality are not just requisite, but inevitable. Fundamentally, King's speech is about vision—the ability to imagine brighter futures, for ourselves and for others.

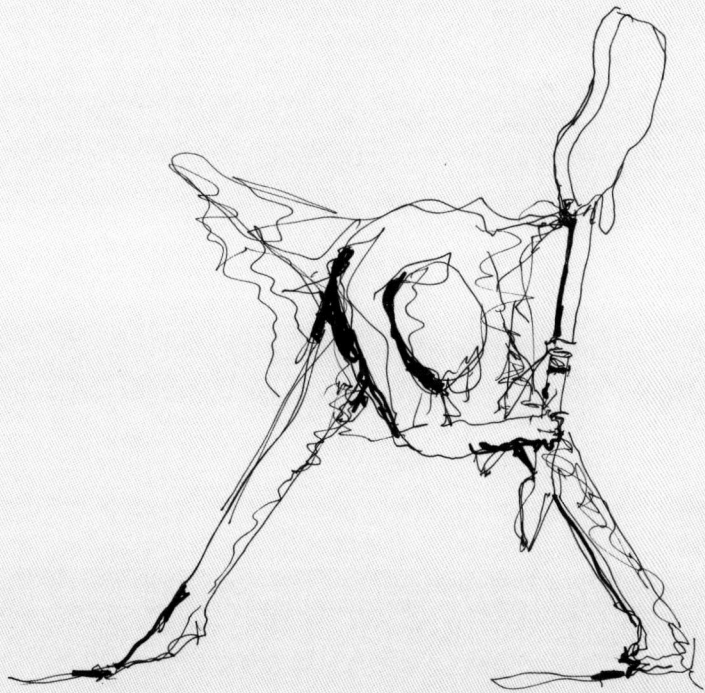

Lines

One of the simplest ways to illustrate a possible future is to draw lines in a desired order on a piece of paper. Our built environment can be seen as a composition of lines that are consciously used to manipulate perspectives, making an object appear as its opposite, light instead of heavy, long instead of short—the intention being related to a myriad of factors such as its standing in relation to its surroundings and aesthetic tastes. In maps, two lines, longitude and latitude, lock down our position in the world, but even a single line, however light it may be, helps us to define where we are within an open space. Think, for instance, how the flowing lines of the roof for the Olympic Stadium in Munich make it appear as if it barely has any mass at all.

Nomad Chair
Galerie Maria Wettergren
1994

In 1994 I was an exchange student at the Rietveld Academie in Amsterdam. The curriculum was very free and allowed students to work on their own projects, which I thought was great. But living as a student in a new city proved harder than I expected, and involuntarily, moving from flat to flat became like a bimonthly routine for me. I decided to design a chair which I easily could take with me between these temporary living arrangements. It would be the one thing that was permanent in terms of interiors. Instead of "home is where the heart is," this would be "home is where the chair is." I was very motivated and spent all my time in the workshop. I felt that it was a luxury to be able to focus on one single piece and I experimented and adjusted until I finally reached a perfect construction—four sticks on a foundation and a suspended felt textile. Nomad Chair truly was the result of a certain place and the specific conditions there, and although I did not know it then, this piece meant the start of my career.

Flying Carpet
sofa, Cappellini
1998

I was so satisfied with my Nomad Chair (1994) that I continued to develop it into a sofa. A wider piece but with the same core principle: that it could be dismantled and carried away. I went back into the workshop and for a long time tried out different angles, spring steel frames and ways to make the felt, until all aspects were optimal. When you sit or lay in Flying Carpet there is a gentle, constant movement that gives you a feeling of weightlessness, a feeling some dream about, and a quality which differs from most furniture. This became my first furniture to be produced by a company, and probably is the product that I am most recognized for.

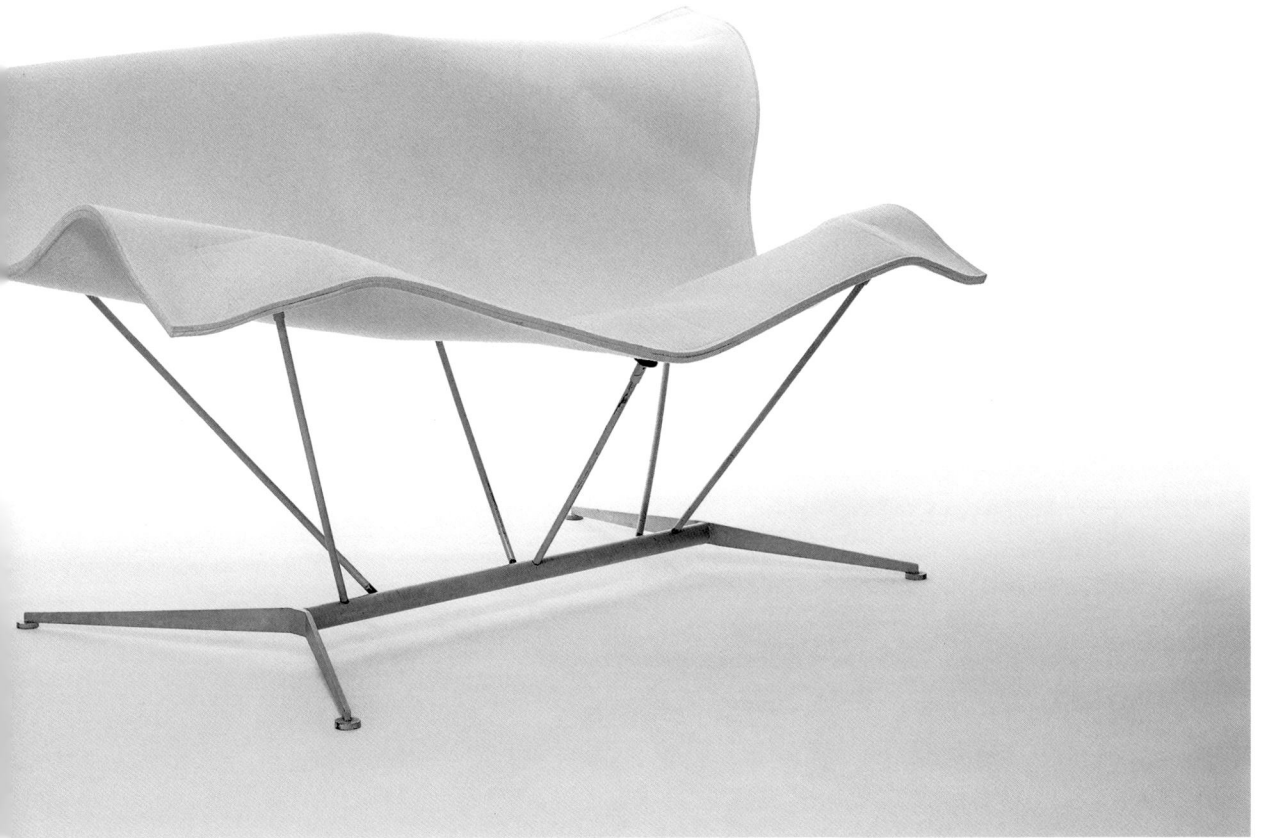

Twiggy
tables, with Raffaella Mangiarotti,
Woodnotes
2012

For exhibitions and photos, carpets depend on furniture to give them context, and a sense of scale, and this is one of the reasons why this Finnish paper yarn company, known for their woven carpets, also make their own furniture. The brief that Raffaella and I assigned ourselves was to create a table that would keep their carpets as visible as possible and also connect to the company name. Working with wood is always delicate because it needs a certain amount of mass to be rigid and not break. But a table such as this is expected to withstand the amount of pressure equivalent to a vase, some books and a coffee cup, so this enabled us to design a very light wooden structure. The vertical supports that hold up the frame with glass are positioned at the corners of the table, but instead of constructing diagonals next to them, which normally is done for stability, we made them meet in the center of the piece instead. This achieved maximum strength while also creating a new separated structure that defines a space you usually find empty under the table.

Dots

lamps, with Raffaella Mangiarotti,
Saas Instruments
2024

This light was made as part of an interior for a small "sartoria"—a men's tailoring store—in Como, Italy. We needed light in three different areas of the store, which all had different dimensions, and we wanted all areas to have the same kind of light. For this reason we designed a modular system which could be retracted or extended to fit perfectly. A lot of light in stores today is hidden because the LED technology enables it, but we wanted to make the light source visible as an aesthetic object in its own right. The construction is designed so that all downward light comes from two levels which spreads the light nicely, and the top level also helps highlight the structure. The electrical wiring is hidden in the structure which is made in copper, brass, stainless steel or painted. And the overall shape is derived from the world of a tailor: the zigzag pattern on the fabric, a thread, a needle.

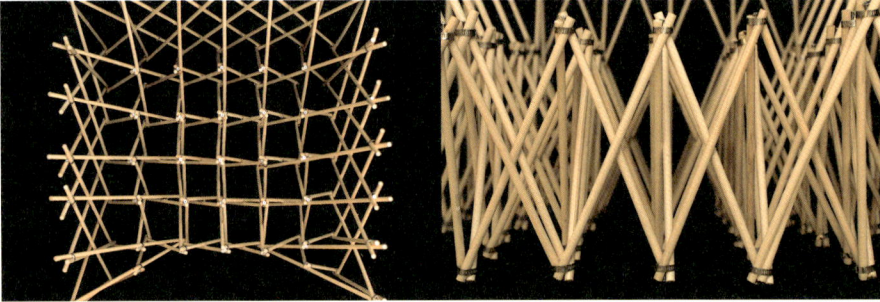

This exercise started in my studio without a clear aim, with only the set parameter of using sticks and cable ties to build something. It became a thing in the studio which someone would pick up and play with whenever there was some free time, and slowly a grid emerged out of the pile of sticks. Generally, I approach my design tasks physically, making sketches with pen and paper and then building a model with my hands before considering approaching the computer. But in this case, there was no original sketch to depart from and the only time we did make a sketch was to communicate an idea to someone else in the studio. Each stick was attached at both ends to another stick, and the game became how to expand the structure while tightening the cable ties so the joints would not flex. This intuitive way of building directly in a one-to-one scale is very different from working with a client that has a specific need and deadline. It is sheer experimentation, and it needs some discipline since no one is asking for it, but over a period of two years this eventually became an armchair. This is one of those processes in which you make happy discoveries, learn something unexpected, and one I wish I would be able to do on a regular basis. But managing time somehow gets harder and harder and more often the experiments I do start end up longer and longer on the shelf. At one point some clients of Galerie Maria Wettergren saw it and wanted it, and it got developed into a properly made armchair and also a sofa.

Stick Chair
Galerie Maria Wettergren
2015–2021

This collection for Galerie Pascale in Stockholm is based on one asymmetrical shape, and consists of a mirror, a brooch and a side table. Even though they all have the same shape, placing several tables in different angels in relation to each other make them appear as if they are all slightly different. Three distinct, jet-black metal legs shoot up from the ground to hold the tabletop. These legs are intertwined at the top and creates a rigid joint that hides the welding spot.

Stones
table, Galerie Pascale
2009

Loop
chair, Fornasarig
2007

On occasion I have been asked to design a wooden chair and each time I have been hesitant. The reason for this is that I think it is a very difficult task. The wooden chair has been developed over a long period of time, and there is a remarkable history of architects and designers who have pushed the potential of the material to its limit through various techniques. In the process it has left less and less opportunity for further innovations, ultimately making the output in this segment looking more or less the same. Over the years I have had many sketches of wooden chairs on my desk that I for different reasons never finished, and so it is reasonable to say that I thought about Loop for a long time before it got made. My main idea for a wooden chair has always centered around lightness, a rational construction that utilizes the quality of wood in an advanced way. Loop uses the force of the diagonal to its fullest extent, and in many ways, it is influenced by the classic folding chair which I always have considered embodies the cleverest way to achieve a light wooden construction. So with Loop I felt I had contributed with something new. As a commissioned designer you have a responsibility to create a meaningful object that can make money for the company, so that their investment is justified. However sometimes it does not work, and you do not know why. I thought that I had made the most wonderful thing in the world, but in the end, nobody bought it. But despite the lack of commercial success, I still felt Loop was a success for me.

Lines and Marhaba
textile patterns, Marimekko
2007

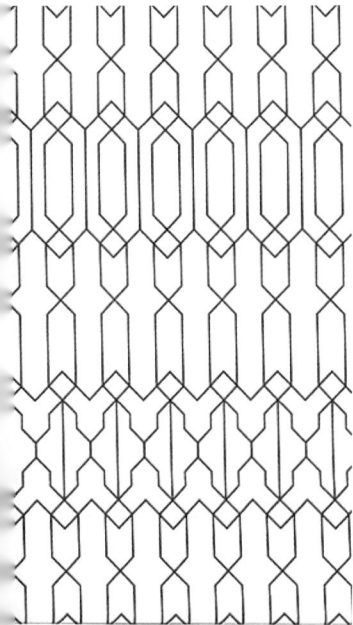

When Marimekko wanted to extend their reach beyond the home to include the contract market, they engaged architects who were familiar with spatial design in public spaces to create patterns for them. Anyone who works with Marimekko knows their heritage and relates to it in different ways. Historically there have been two main directions within their collection, one is the patterns with large colourful flowers and the other is the stripes, and I felt I wanted to contribute to the later. In one way I think architects and artists deal with the same thing because both of them have to find the right proportions between positive and negative space. Besides this being determined by a technical framework, this is also related to finding an aesthetic rhythm, just compare a graphic pattern and a building façade with windows. In Marhaba the stripes were traditionally placed with equal proportions of space, but in Lines I made the space between them unequal, and finding the right amount of space—that was the art. *Marhaba*—equivalent to "hello" in Arabic—is inspired by the Arabic world. In Islam you are not allowed to make an image of a living thing, but beauty remains essential for most cultures and so this becomes expressed through mathematical patterns, and that is what I have looked at. Both Lines and Marhaba are made with a line that has the same width so you easily can combine the two patterns anyway you want.

Approaching Nothing

———

Jamer Hunt

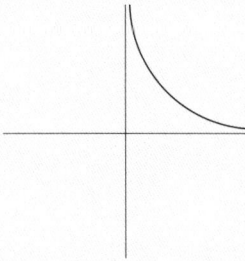

A line describes a curve. That line approaches zero......but it never quite gets there.

In mathematics this line, to be a line, must have no real meaningful mass. Its thickness is only implied and irrelevant. While we may perceive it from a trace of graphite or a stripe of ink on the page—or pixels on a screen—its own properties are beside the point. Immaterial, its form comes from making visible the mathematical description of the curve. Its embodiment is not what tells the story.

As this "asymptote" narrows the space between itself and the coordinate grid, however, surprisingly human narratives abound in that thinning of the gap: How close can I get to perfection? What does it mean to strive for something? What will be left of me when I reach the end? There is an almost unbearable, human tension that flickers as the line gets closer and closer and closer—but never reaches home, never crosses the zero line, never becomes one with nothing. And it never crosses over into the unknown. Surprisingly, the mathematical simplicity of the asymptotic line can launch all-too-human questions.

A different line describes a curve. This curve intersects with another and another. A sinuous, continuous stroke of ink traces curves, whorls and wandering lines. The whole feels chaotic, with few obvious features or discernible figures. From this tangle, however, an image does begin to emerge. It is of a couple seated on a cloud, suspended from the ground (page 137).

Material lines tell different, more quotidian, human stories. Rather than describe a mathematical abstraction, a scribed line can embody potential energy, as if math gives way to physics gives way to life. A line can express the dream of lounging on a cloud with a loved one—at ease, peaceful and convivial. It can take the form of a golden thread wound and rewound around the finger each day, a reminder of the ties that bind (page 15). Lines can be woven together into a warp and weft that not only captures and refracts light, but also tells a story of new possibilities for expert hands (page 74).

Bundle these lines together and they can support us as we rest our tired legs or draw ourselves around a dinner table to eat together (page 126). Stagger these lines into an alternating rhythm—present, absent, present, absent, present, absent and so on—and suddenly solid walls become porous. Or the inverse: light becomes material. The outside and the inside become one, as if the limit we try to uphold between them has become permeable or transparent (page 86). In other words, as lines become material, they can assemble into forms that give shape to the very-human activities of everyday life: lighting, lounging, living and loving.

Between these two kinds of lines—abstract and material—a universe of possibilities is to be found. Mathematics is, in the end, an abstraction. While it may take form in graphite or pixels, its visible result is only a representational strategy meant to capture a deeper truth. As abstractions, mathematical formulae and equations exist to describe the world as we might know it, in the perfection of parabolas, arcs, curves and planes. Remarkably, though, that same abstract math can reveal the existence of black holes and quantum mechanics—phenomena that may be invisible to the naked eye but are very much there. Imagine describing the universe over time, its present and its past, with variables and functions and equations. These do not, however, give us a place to sit down or a table to tuck into. They don't subtly frame an ocean view or provide shelter from winds off the Baltic Sea (page 85).

How does one capture the dazzling abstraction of math, the human tensions in the asymptote, and the breathtaking lightness of a transcendent idea? For that to happen, the line must become form, as when it becomes a sketch, or a strut or a slat. Is this not the job of design? To take a glimmer of an idea, materialize it through the lines of sketch, and turn that two-dimensional representation into a knowable, three-dimensional form? What then separates this process as visual poetry from lumpen tables and over-wrought chairs is how it evolves.

Minimalism is one thing, but lightness is something altogether different. In the Venn diagram of their areas, there is a generous overlap. But what lightness seeks is something altogether more profound—heavy even. Lightness, as an idea materialized, fades asymptotically towards nothing. Perhaps its power is that in its advance toward nothingness it reminds us of our sense of human impermanence (what some people have described as a drifting towards the light). Minimalism is a reduction in mass and ornament until only the simplest form remains, like carving a statue out of a block of marble. Carried to its extreme—the removal of all material—a given form would make no sense. Lightness, on the other hand, involves a rethinking of material itself until only the idea remains, held aloft by the least substance, like a cloud suspended from the ground. This lightness seems impossible, and yet there it is in front of our eyes: a ghostly stool emerging from the ashes of an Oedipal fire (page 102); a flower stem floating within the edges of an empty cube (page 9); a carpet held magically aloft.

As an embodied idea approaches nothing—asymptotically— weightier ideas begin to emerge. Lightness thrums in that space between abstraction and physical form, between the asymptote and the graphite line. There we may discover love and companionship; the fragile beauty of a cut flower; light itself frozen into visible form (page 57). But we need that imperfect line to help us understand the finality and the promise of the known world and to give meaning to our own lightness.

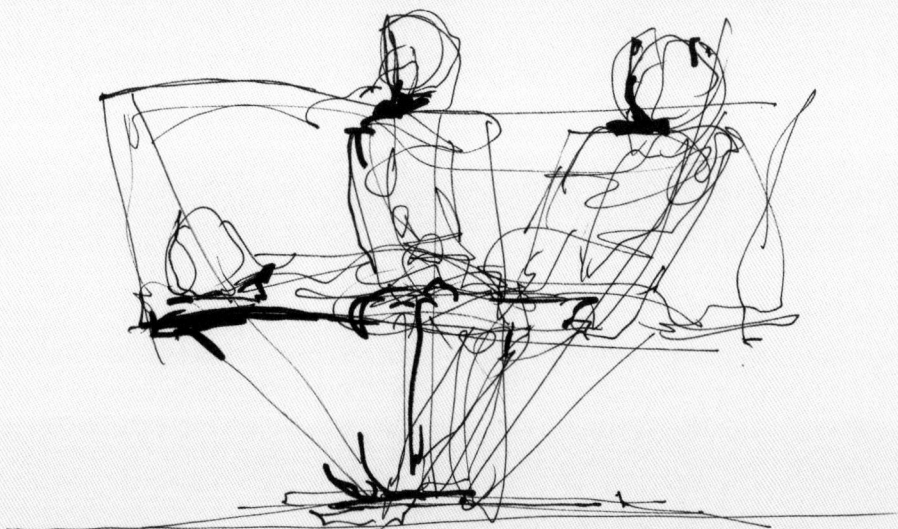

Biography
Ilkka Suppanen

1968	Born in Kotka, Finland
1995	Studio Suppanen Helsinki
2007	Studio Suppanen Milan

Education

1988–1994	Architecture at Technical University of Helsinki
1989–1993	Interior and Furniture Design at University of Art and Design in Helsinki
1994	Gerrit Rietveld Academie in Amsterdam

Selected awards

2024	Ulrica Hydman Vallien Foundation Prize, Sweden
2020	Kaj Franck Design Prize, Finland
2019	ADI Index Award, Italy
2018	Good Design Award, Chicago, USA
2017	Good Design Award, Chicago, USA
2015	Torsten and Wanja Söderberg Prize, Sweden
2015	Finnish Cultural Foundation Prize, Finland
2015	Ilmari Tapiovaara Prize, Finland
2013	Interior Innovation Award, IMM Cologne, Germany
2012	Red Dot Design Award, Best of the Best, Germany
2008	Good Design Award, USA
2008	Fennia Prize, Finland
2006	Bruno Mathsson Award, Sweden
2001	Avotakka Award, Finland
2001	Young Designer of the Year Prize, with Harri Koskinen, Finland
1998	Nominee of Dedalus Prize, nominated by Ettore Sottsass, Italy
1998	Young Designer of the Year, Architektur & Wohnen-prize, awarded by Ingo Maurer, Germany
1998	Finnish National Award for Young Art, Finland
1995	Habitare Prize, 1st Price at student competition, Alessandro Mendini as jury, Finland

Selected exhibitions

2024	*Bruno + 35 Mathsson Prize Winners,* Sven-Harrys Konstmuseum, Sweden
2024	*Universo Satellite,* Triennale Milano, Italy
2019	*Points of View,* solo exhibition, Gallerie Forsblom, Finland
2017	Solo exhibition Gallerie Maria Wettergren, France
2017	Solo exhibition, Maison Louis Carré, France
2016	Solo exhibition, Design Museum Helsinki, Finland
2015	Solo exhibition, Röhsska musseet, Sweden
2013	*Èclat,* solo exhibition Gallerie Maria Wettergren, France
2012	*Broken,* solo exhibition, Gallerie Forsblom, Finland
2010	*Hirameki,* Ozone Living Design Center Tokyo, Japan
2008	*Hardcore — Contemporary Finnish Design,* Finnish Cultural Institute in New York, USA
2006	*Ilkka Suppanen + Harri Koskinen* exhibition, Design Museum Helsinki, Finland
2005–2007	SAUMA, Washington DC, New York City, Los Angeles, USA
2003	*The Q exhibition* in Tokyo, Japan
2001	*Workspheres,* MoMA, USA
2000	*Hothouse,* Biennale Interieur Kortrijk, Belgium
1998	*Modern Finnish Design,* Bard Graduate Center, USA
1997	*Snowcrash,* Milan Design Week, Italy
1992	*5th International Exhibition of Architecture,* La Biennale Di Venezia, Italy

Represented in

Centre Pompidou, Paris, France
Design Museum, Helsinki, Finland
Indianapolis Museum of Art, USA
MoMA, New York, USA
Nasjonalmuseet, Oslo, Norway
Nationalmuseum, Stockholm, Sweden
Röhsska museet, Gothenburg, Sweden
Stedelijk Museum, Amsterdam, The Netherlands

Contributors

Max Borka

is a curator, critic and lecturer in art and design. His work particularly explores their intersection with the sciences and social and environmental concerns, across a wide variety of platforms. These include *State of DESIGN, Berlin* and *Mapping the Design World*, initiatives of which he was the founder and director, the Biennale Interieur in Kortrijk, Belgium, and Berlin Design Week, which he also directed. He has also written numerous books and articles, and was a co-founder of *DAMN° Magazine*. He was a lecturer at the Schools of Arts in Ghent, Brussels, and Potsdam-Berlin.

Stefana Broadbent

is an associate professor at the Politecnico di Milano in the department of design. Broadbent was head of collective intelligence at Nesta (2014–2016), UK's innovation agency, and was previously a lecturer in digital anthropology at University College London where she led the master's in digital anthropology.

Dai Fujiwara

is the founder and creative director of DAI&Co. He started the A-POC clothing project with Issey Miyake in 1998 and was the vice president of Miyake Design Studio. Fujiwara is a professor at Tama Art University, visiting professor at the Graduate School of Kanazawa College of Art and researcher at University of Tokyo's Institute of Industrial Science.

Sara Heinämaa

is professor of philosophy in the Department of Social Sciences and Philosophy at University of Jyväskylä, and docent of theoretical philosophy at the University of Helsinki. Heinämaa has published multiple research articles and worked for many international philosophical institutions, with assignments including her role as a subject editor for the *Stanford Encyclopedia of Philosophy* since 2018.

Leon Hidalgo

is an architect with a masters from the Technische Universität Berlin (2024). He studied at Bergen School of Architecture and previously graduated from Münster School of Architecture (2021). He began the visual investigation of invisible forces via the account @lightweight_structures on Instagram in 2021.

Jamer Hunt

was the founding director of the graduate program in transdisciplinary design at Parsons School of Design (2009–2015). He currently serves as program director for university curriculum at The New School, New York. In addition to many articles and two co-authored books on design, he is most recently the author of *Not to Scale* (2020).

Gustaf Kjellin

is a curator and writer. In 2023 Kjellin founded Gus Gallery in Stockholm. He was the curator of the exhibition Snowcrash: 1997–2023 at the Nationalmuseum, Sweden (2021). Recent books he has written and edited include *Claesson Koivisto Rune—In Transit* (2024), *Kåge/Hamada* (2022), *Architect Erik Lundberg–Light and Form* (2021) and *Design & Peace* (2019).

Toshiko Mori

is Robert P. Hubbard Professor in the Practice of Architecture at the Harvard University Graduate School of Design, where she also was chair of the Department of Architecture (2002–2008). Mori is the founder and principal of Toshiko Mori Architect (1981) and her recent work includes masterplans for the Brooklyn Public Library Central Branch and Axel Springer Haus US headquarters, both in New York.

Maria Cecilia Loschiavo dos Santos

is a philosopher and an associate professor of design at the School of Architecture and Urbanism, University of São Paulo, and a scientific consultant for Brazilian research agencies. She is the author of several books, including *Brazilian Modern Furniture* (1995), and the screenwriter of the documentary *A Margem da Imagem* (2003).

Written and edited by	Ilkka Suppanen and Gustaf Kjellin
Contributing writers	Max Borka, Stefana Broadbent, Dai Fujiwara, Sara Heinämaa,
	Leon Hidalgo, Jamer Hunt, Toshiko Mori, Maria Cecilia
	Loschiavo dos Santos
Design	Kenya Hara+Megumi Kajiwara
Copyediting / proofreading	George MacBeth
Publishing coordination	Emilia Maier
Illustrations	Ilkka Suppanen
Printed by	SunM Color Co., Ltd., Japan
Bookbinding	Shinohara Shiko Ltd., Japan

Photography: Jens Andersson pp. 22–23, 26–27, 119–121; Jörg Bräuer p. 103;
Sander Copier p. 64; Lars Hallen pp. 85–87; Jussi Hyttinen p. 25;
Francesca Ferrari pp. 58, 60; JKMM architects p. 90; Diego Lazzarini pp. 54–55;
Marco Magoga p. 45; Marco Melander p. 92; Sameli Rantanen pp. 109, 122–123, 132–133;
Studio Suppanen pp. 14, 24, 29–30, 88, 95, 100, 126–127, 129;
Ilkka Suppanen pp. 72–73, 102; Jussi Tiainen pp. 57, 88–89;
Tom Vack p. 125; Miro Zagnoli pp. 8–9, 12, 15, 82–83, 104–105.
Pp. 88–89, Exhibition Camouflage, artworks by Hannaleena Heiska.

Unless otherwise stated, images originate from the respective manufacturer.

Lars Müller Publishers is supported by the Swiss Federal Office of Culture
with a structural contribution for the years 2021–2025.

Lars Müller Publishers
Pfingstweidstrasse 6
8005 Zurich, Switzerland
+41 44 274 37 40
info@lars-mueller-publishers.com
www.lars-mueller-publishers.com

Product safety
Producer: Lars Müller Publishers GmbH
Responsible person in accordance with EU Regulation
2023/988 (GPSR): Michael Klein, sales representative,
Hub 1, DE-84149 Velden, +49 8742 964 552 2, gpsr@lars-mueller-publishers.com

ISBN 978-3-03778-779-3

Distributed in North America, Latin America and
the Caribbean by ARTBOOK | D.A.P.
www.artbook.com

Printed in Japan